Washington and Other Memories

Books by Sir Arthur Willert

ASPECTS OF BRITISH FOREIGN POLICY

WHAT NEXT IN EUROPE?

THE EMPIRE IN THE WORLD:
A STUDY IN LEADERSHIP AND RECONSTRUCTION
 (WITH B. K. LONG AND H. V. HODSON)

THE ROAD TO SAFETY:
A STUDY IN ANGLO-AMERICAN RELATIONS

WASHINGTON AND OTHER MEMORIES

SIR ARTHUR WILLERT

WASHINGTON

AND OTHER MEMORIES

HOUGHTON MIFFLIN COMPANY BOSTON 1972

First Printing c

ISBN: 0-395-12727-0
Library of Congress Catalog Card Number: 74-162013
Printed in the United States of America

Contents

Washington and Other Memories

CHAPTER 1

The Beginnings

A SMALL BOY playing in the summer sunshine of 1887 on the lawn of his parents' house on the top of Headington Hill, outside Oxford, was suddenly conscious of a distant booming behind the familiar sounds of garden and country. He would soon have forgotten all about it had his father not impressed upon him never to forget it as it was the guns of the Fleet at Spithead, saluting Queen Victoria on her Golden Jubilee.

I was then just five years old and this was the first impact upon my life of the great outer world. It was an appropriate impact. Queen Victoria's first Jubilee can fairly be considered as the culmination of the power and glory of the British Empire with the subsequent decline of which my life, in journalism and in the Foreign Office, has in one way or another been connected.

My father was a don at Oxford — he was not the usual sort of don. Here is what a colleague in the common room of Exeter College had to say about him:

> Paul Willert was perhaps the most popular man on our staff both in college and outside, with the young as with the old. He had a sunny and genial temperament and manner, a delicate sense

of humour and imperturbable good temper. He was passionately devoted to the "Sport of Kings," and, as he had a private fortune, he could afford to keep good hunters; and he arranged with himself — but not with the college — to give himself a free hunting day each week. As he was a tutor that might have brought him into some friction with our senior tutor who had austere views of a tutor's duty; and certainly he frowned upon Willert's sporting absences. But, as Willert never took any notice of anybody's frowns but only went on his way rejoicing, there was no friction; and this habit endeared him to the younger world of undergraduates and brought fresh air into our common room and breezy tales from the hunting field. He married a very gifted lady and for many years in their charming home on Headington Hill, they helped the social life of the college.*

"No one ever enjoyed his friendship without recognising the rare charm of his personality," wrote *The Times* after his death.

I followed my father to Eton and Oxford. At Eton I spent five years of happy medocrity and one final year of useful tuition. I was proficient enough at games to enjoy them and not good enough for enjoyment to be marred by the dust and sweat of emulation. I was irked by no long-range ambitions. No speculation about religion or the significance of the universe troubled my animal serenity. I was not stupid; my mind was quick and my memory good. But I was always ready to break off from my studies to play or talk or read trash. For those five years I worked just enough to avoid unpleasantness. Then in my last year I came under the influence of a young master to whom, as I was glad to be able to tell him many years later, I owed to no slight degree my quick ascent of the ladder of journalism. This master was C. K. Marten, as we boys called him, better known afterward as Sir Henry Marten, Vice Provost of Eton. He taught history, and until he took me in hand history

* *An Oxonian Looks Back* by Louis R. Farnell, Martins Hopkinson Ltd., 1934.

had meant little more than a disjointed series of facts, dates, names, and battles. Marten took those dull bones, built them up into a symmetrical skeleton, and clothed the skeleton with living flesh. He kindled my interest in contemporary politics and made me see that to understand the present one must study the past. He taught that serious reading could be found in the daily press and set essays that demanded its study. He prodded curiosity and courted questions and discussion. The most inspiring of my Eton hours were spent in his sunny rooms in Weston's Yard.

Even without Marten's influence Eton would have helped me in journalism. Endless translation from Latin and Greek into English and vice versa taught me to express myself on paper with rough facility. Its system of saying lessons, which meant quickly learning thirty lines of Virgil or Horace and keeping them in one's mind for an hour or so, enabled me later on to recall conversations pretty well word for word until I was back at my desk. Even my laziness helped me. My efforts at producing an impression of tolerable industry with a minimum of trouble developed a knack of plausible superficiality that often disguised the inadequacy of knowledge that lay behind my newspaper work.

At Oxford, or rather at Balliol, I came more to the front; and this, though I did not know it at the time, opened for me the door to journalism — I was made secretary to our commemoration ball. On my committee was a young don, Harold Hartley, afterward well known in the world of science and big business. My handling of the literature we put out impressed him to the extent of his suggesting to my father that my future might lie in journalism. My parents had wanted me to try to become a diplomat. This did not appeal to me. I doubted my ability to pass the necessary examination, and I wanted to be in possession of a modest salary as soon as possible at a time when diplomacy still paid practically nothing to its beginners. I wanted this because I was secretly engaged to a girl called Florence Simpson (henceforth designated as "F."). She was the granddaughter of Sir James Young Simpson, the discoverer of chloroform. Her brother "Tim" Simpson (listed in *Who's Who* as Sir James Simpson, Bart.) was a great Oxford and Eton friend — through him we came together. Hence I opted for journalism.

I had my way and my father wrote to Arthur Walter, then still the chief proprietor of *The Times*. He was told that *The Times* would give me an opening as a foreign correspondent, but that I should be paid nothing for my first year as a probationer.

CHAPTER 2

The Times—European Apprenticeship

I ENTERED Printing House Square for the first time on a gloomy afternoon late in October 1905 to keep an introductory appointment with Arthur Walter.

I had imagined newspaper offices to be vibrant, utilitarian, and intimidating; Printing House Square was sleepy, restful, and reassuring. Its passages and stairs recalled one of the more ancient boys' houses at school on a fine afternoon when everybody was on the playing fields or river. Arthur Walter resembled an elderly country gentleman (which he was in his spare time) rather than my conception of the head of a great newspaper. He put me in a chair and talked about my father. He asked why I wanted to be a journalist and received my carefully rehearsed answer. Was I prepared to work first for a few months at Printing House Square and then in the Paris and Berlin offices? I said I was ready to start at once. He sent me to see Moberly Bell, the manager of *The Times* and its real "boss." I found a strong, substantial man with a large pale face and a commanding nose at a mahogany desk. He was swathed in a frock coat and wore a Gladstonian collar. He limped a little when he rose to dismiss me. I cannot recall what we talked about or whether I saw him again in the course of this sojourn in Printing House Square. Later on I was to have two dramatic compliments from him and much kindness.

Next day I reported to Valentine Chirol, the Foreign Editor. Chirol, with the exception of his predecessor, Sir Donald Mackenzie Wallace, who walked with kings, was, I suppose, the leading international journalist of the period. He was as familiar with Bombay as with Berlin. He had had a brief career in the Foreign Office early in life and *The Times* profited from his friendships there, for the Foreign Office was still shy of the generality of journalists. It had no News Department, no effective system for the routine giving out of news. Twenty years later it fell to me to make the arrangements for the press to witness the signing of the Locarno Pact. When I discussed them with the chief office keeper he commented sadly upon the changing times. "Why," he said, "when I first came here the gentlemen of the press waited in the courtyard, and when there was anything for them, it was given them: and when there wasn't, they were sent away."

Chirol, like the other leaders of the old regime of *The Times*, failed to survive the reforms by which Northcliffe a few years later shattered the peace of Printing House Square and rescued the paper from senile decay. My memory of Chirol in his *Times* days is of a quiet, nervous man, writing fluent articles on small slips of paper and smoking in an amber holder a succession of cigarettes. When contraried, he threw back his head and showed the whites of his eyes like an obstinate horse.

Chirol was easy with his subordinates. But we suspected that the editor, Buckle, sometimes found him difficult. No two men could have been less alike. Chirol was on the small side; Buckle a towering figure of a man, bulky and full-blooded, with a beard as aggressively prominent as Chirol's was restrained. His great laugh rang out as he walked around the office and the floor shook under his tread. He was a Fellow of All Souls and would have made a good head of an Oxford college: as vice-chancellor he would have been magnificently impressive. Chirol was the fastidious diplomat; he was veiled; his great knowledge was encased in reticence. Buckle was frank and forthright. Like Moberly Bell, both men were dedicated to *The Times*.

The two men who helped me most during those first weeks were J. W. Flanagan, the chief leader writer, and Walter Scott. With Flanagan, Balliol, where I think he had been a scholar, was my first point of contact. To me he appeared an unkempt, elderly figure (he cannot have been much more than fifty) as he shuffled into our room on carpet slippers and wearing a ragged cardigan. His hair was tousled and gray, his face pale and tired; a pipe protruded from under a ragged mustache. His eyes were piercingly intelligent and good nature and humor flickered in them. His voice evoked both Dublin and Oxford. I hung upon his words for his knowledge of affairs was wide and accurate. He was an Irishman of the south but a Protestant and an ardent Unionist. Nothing fazed him. When asked to write upon an unfamiliar subject he would, with the help of newspaper cuttings and other papers and, perhaps, a living expert or two, quickly produce an article lucidly omniscient. He sat at a table in a small room drinking soda water from a syphon and sent his handwritten leaders down slip by slip to be set up. I do not remember whether he waited to see the proofs or left that to the editor or Chirol, but each night he would disappear at about the same time in a hansom cab, which awaited him in the yard. I learned much from him at the time; and in later years I valued his occasional letter in his strong handwriting. He generally wrote for information and paid for it in advance in kind.

Scott was an earnest and unambitious man, with a taste for modest good living, who, like Flanagan, by keeping in the background, survived the Northcliffian explosions and became to me and doubtless to other correspondents an invaluable agent and friend. I was surprised, indeed, when I scanned the index of *The Times History* not to find his name in it for he was a by no means negligible wheel in the machinery of the office.

I did little more that first time than hang about and learn, listening to discussions in Chirol's room in particular. I recall only one contribution of any note, and that a negative one, which I made to the production of the paper. Buckle and Chirol were deciding to publish the first of a couple of articles (I forget on what subject) when I intervened to say that I had read them that afternoon as a single article in the *Strand Magazine* in a Turkish bath. The articles were "spiked" and I was thanked. Long afterward I told Northcliffe of this incident. "Yes," he commented, "that was the sort of thing I had to put up with from them." Printing House Square soon got back at me. A short Reuters telegram came in from India reporting that the viceroy had been slightly bitten by a dog. I headed it "The Viceroy and the Dog," but discovered next morning that the editor had substituted "Lord Minto."

I had a kindred rebuke from Scott when I suggested beer in a Fleet Street "pub." *The Times*, he said, did not mix with Fleet Street. The truth, though I did not at first realize it, was that *The Times* might well have benefited by mixing with Fleet Street instead of rotting in a Victorian backwater remote from the rising flow of Edwardian journalism. Three years later, when Northcliffe was beginning to propel it into the mainstream, we juniors still boycotted Fleet Street and patronized a respectable hotel on the Embankment looking across to Blackfriars Bridge if we wanted to feed or drink in the vicinity. As for the Press Club, it was not until I joined the Foreign Office that I entered it.

After about six weeks in London I proceeded to Paris. I had found the atmosphere of Printing House Square very congenial and admired the people at the top. I had discovered that if I could land an assistant correspondentship in one of the big capitals, F. and I would be able to marry. But it might, I felt, be depressingly long before a vacancy occurred, even if in the meantime I became fit to occupy it. I should, indeed, have been surprised had I then been told that the coveted salary would be mine within eighteen months, and utterly incredulous had I further been told that almost exactly four years hence *The Times* would give me as a Christmas present its Washington correspondentship.

I reached Paris soon after Christmas on a winter evening. The streets were cold, dry, bright, and busy and rang with cries of *L'Intransigeant, La Presse*. I felt exhilarated, and, after leaving my things in a small hotel in the Rue de Richelieu, treated myself to a good dinner at Weber's. Next day I presented myself to the head of the Paris office, William Lavino. Lavino had known my father when they were both young. My father had written to him and had been told that I should be well received.

Lavino, after representing *The Times* in Vienna, had come to Paris a few years before to succeed the famous de Blowitz who, he said, had left the affairs of the office in a formidable mess. Scott had told me that his knowledge of Europe was as good as that of Mackenzie Wallace or Chirol and that he was a better journalist than either. He may well have been right. Anyhow Lavino taught me more than anyone else about my future job and then found me the opportunity to put his teaching into effect. He died prematurely and never saw the quick result of his tuition. My gratitude to him remains profound.

When I called at the office of *The Times* in the Chaussée
d'Antin, I was shown into a sleek, well-groomed room, with a
thick carpet and solid mahogany, comfortable, leather-cov-
ered chairs. Lavino was seated behind a desk that reflected his
shining linen. A frock coat was revealed as he rose to welcome
me. This was his usual costume. He felt that the important
respectability of his newspaper demanded it. "Of course, if
you want to be taken for a tourist and have every pimp on
the Boulevards after you, you are suitably dressed, but for a
member of *The Times* staff . . ." Such was the reception accorded to me a few weeks later when one Sunday evening I
presented myself in a Harris Tweed suit after a day in the For-
est of Fontainebleau. Not that I was expected to wear a frock
coat (I never at any stage of my life possessed one) or even a
tail coat; something subfusc was good enough for assistants.

After the usual formalities of welcome, Lavino took me out to
lunch. He asked me where I was going to live. I told him
and he approved. He asked me if I knew anyone in Paris. I said
that I had a few introductions. He hoped they were to French
people. I said they were and added that I had a friend at the
British Embassy. "Well," he said, "don't let him know that
you are here. You are here to learn about Europe and France
and about being a correspondent. The young embassy people
won't help you. Diplomats are like claret. They mature
slowly and often excellently; but they are not much good at
first." Next day my education started, and it started from the
bottom. I was given some extracts from newspapers to trans-
late. I submitted my effort to Lavino. He approved the matter
but not the form. My handwriting was not clear enough. "A
press telegram must have every letter formed so that a half-
witted foreign telegraph clerk, ignorant of English, can trans-
mit it accurately." In these days that was indeed essential.
The portable typewriter, if born at all, was still in its infancy.

My handwriting never approached the clarity of that of Lavino and other veterans, partly because I took to a typewriter fairly soon and partly because the American telegraph office clerks were brilliant decypherers of doubtful writing.

My next lesson concerned style. I had concocted what I thought was a bright little message. Lavino would not have it. He told me never to strain after effect but to write clearly and compactly (Northcliffe used to say that the greatest story ever written — the first chapter of Genesis — took but 800 words) and to avoid unusual words. "Write as to an aunt in the country and not a particularly clever one at that." Willmott Lewis, my successor at Washington, also aimed at old women; but they lived in Brighton boarding houses. My target later on was my editor and my chief proprietor — not a bad one, perhaps, consisting as it did of Fleet Street and All Souls College.

No *Times* correspondent, Lavino said, must ever take notes during an interview. Upon this he was absolutely and rightly insistent; and thanks to my good short-term Etonian memory his advice was easy for me to follow. What other technical guidance did he give me? He insisted on the need for absolute discretion. Never reveal the names of confidential informants, not even to Printing House Square. This was good advice for the working journalist, but, as a writer of reminiscences, I wish that I had followed it less faithfully. Some of my private letters to Printing House Square would be more revealing had I been less mysterious about forgotten sources.

Many of Lavino's lectures were delivered as I accompanied him on his morning walks. Sometimes I would leave him at the door of a great man or of a government office; sometimes we would shop and return to his flat with delicacies for the kitchen, for he liked his food and was in the habit of giving small bachelor lunches to which he often asked me. I learned much at his table. His friends were mostly diplomats or politicians from all over Europe. Their names I forget. I suppose I was more interested in their information I collected than in their personalities.

At Oxford and still more in Printing House Square I had realized that Germany was making a nuisance of herself, throwing her weight about in Africa and so on. But I had been brought up in the Victorian pro-German tradition. Germany was akin to us; she had helped us at Waterloo; she was a comfortable country to travel in; the Rhine was romantic; her music wonderful. So, like many of my contemporaries, I was inclined to excuse her vagaries on the grounds that she had come late into the race beweeen the Great Powers and was merely hustling with rough inexperience to make up for lost time. Lavino put me right about this. Germany could not be our friend; she was jealous of us; she had consolidated herself by three wars; she would fight again, to dominate Europe and destroy the British Empire, unless Britain deserted her isolationist tradition and took over the leadership of Europe. We must make a defensive military alliance with France and Russia or war was inevitable sooner or later. The Franco-British *entente cordiale,* for which Lavino had worked hard in *The Times* and behind the scenes, was something, but not enough.

As a matter of fact the ill wind from across the Rhine served me well. The Kaiser not long before had swaggered ashore at Tangier. He wanted to thwart France in Morocco (in which he failed), to weaken the Anglo-French *entente* (in which he failed), and to strengthen Germany in Africa (in which he succeeded). A crisis followed, and then a conference at Algeciras. Sir Donald Mackenzie Wallace passed through Paris on his way to Spain to report it for *The Times*. He radiated importance and infallibility. He had been private secretary to a viceroy of India, had bear-led around India a future

(and last) tsar of Russia, had been secretary to the future King
and Queen of England on an imperial progress, assistant to de
Blowitz at the Congress of Berlin nearly thirty years before, and
was one of the people King Edward VII consulted on foreign
problems. I remember well his entry into the office, rotund,
gray-headed, authoritative. Before Lavino took him off to lunch
there was some discussion about Algeciras and *Times* policy
and again I was impressed by the importance that its principal
servants attached to their newspaper in the affairs of nations.
I never saw Mackenzie Wallace again. But it was he who, indirectly, sent me to America.

Some time later Lavino spoke to me about my prospects. He
thought that I had the makings of a correspondent in me but
that, to go to the top, I must specialize: he was where he was
because he had specialized on Central Europe. He had talked
to Mackenzie Wallace about me. They agreed that Europe was
no place for a beginner anymore. It was crowded with special-
ists. America, on the other hand, was coming into the international picture — the dispatch by Theodore Roosevelt of a representative to the Algeciras Conference was a case in point —
she was bound to count for more and more, and she was unex-
ploited by British journalists. *The Times* was about to expand
its organization there. It was looking for a new chief correspondent and was opening an office in Washington where an
assistant would be needed. Why did not Lavino secure the assist-
antship for his protégé? This he did and after a few uneventful
months with George Saunders, *The Times* correspondent in
Berlin, I was in England on my way to the United States.

In Printing House Square I was introduced to my future chief
in Washington. He surprised me. He was utterly different
from the other members of the staff of *The Times*; he was different from anybody I had ever met. He spoke with an American accent, and, though born in England, was an American citi-

zen. He had graduated into American politics and had become a satellite of the Republican Party, rising to be director of the census. He was middle-aged and rather stout. His name was Robert P. Porter and, as I was soon to discover, he was atypical of the transatlantic political hack. He had been editing the Engineering Supplement of *The Times,* but lived in North Oxford, whence he came to visit my parents, flourishing letters he had received from President Theodore Roosevelt and Andrew Carnegie in reply to his announcement of his appointment. My father was not impressed either by the tone of the replies or by their recipient; my mother more than ever feared that journalism was no profession for her son.

CHAPTER 3

Progress in America

I SAILED from Liverpool in the *Campania,* a Cunard ship of only about 12,000 tons but then the company's fastest liner. We ran into an autumn gale off Ireland and I did not appear on deck until we reached the Banks. That was the first and last time I have been seasick. The moment of convalescence is, for some reason or other, a clear-cut cameo of memory. I stood in the smoking room; the door to the deck was open, and I looked through it onto a leaden, heaving sea with a sensation of tentative superiority. I ordered the first cocktail of my life to combat the stuffiness of the dining saloon, where I made a good meal, though the ship was still unsteady enough for the fiddles to remain on the tables.

We entered New York Harbor while the sun was still struggling with the morning mist. Coney Island with its amusement towers and buildings loomed up over the smooth water. Years before I and the rest of my family had been supremely shocked by an American couple in the train traversing the viaduct between the mainland and Venice who exclaimed that the still distant town looked just like Coney Island. I now discovered that the Americans were perceptive realists and not the barbarians we had thought them. Coney Island that misty morning did recall that view of Venice from the viaduct.

Other memories of my first sight of the harbor and the North River are obscured by those of subsequent approaches. There was, of course, no spiked and towering range of tall buildings to make the view of Manhattan Island as dramatic as it is today. There were no really tall buildings. The Flatiron on Madison Square still stood out, and I think the World Building was about the most conspicuous downtown. My diary says:

> I had expected novelty and noise and rush. On the contrary the drive up recalled a quiet Marseilles or Leghorn. The same houses with shutters, the same fruit shops projecting their wares onto the side-walk. A lounging motley lot of passers-by with many South European types among them. The negroes strike the only distinctive note; but there don't seem to be many of them here. The streets are full of holes . . . Took a walk after lunch up Fifth Avenue to the Park. Here clean, bright asphalt streets and a good deal of traffic. Glorious day.

My hotel was the Fifth Avenue Hotel on Madison Square, a solid, old-fashioned place. I was greeted by a friendly housekeeper in rustling black, who showed me the rooms occupied by Edward VII when, as Prince of Wales, he had visited the United States on the eve of the Civil War. In my bedroom I encountered my first fixed basin with running water. I was shocked to discover, in the public drawing room, a pitcher of ice water flanked by a couple of used glasses. It seemed unsanitary. Guests must have fed at a common table, for my diary records the people I sat next to.

Next morning I had called upon Porter and his wife and daughter at the Buckingham Hotel, which then stood next to St. Patrick's Cathedral. After lunching with them, I explored the city. I admired Fifth Avenue:

> It is [I wrote] a far finer street than any in Berlin. It lacks the planned symmetry of the rue de Rivoli or Regent Street (still

Nash's). Its buildings are of moderate height; but their great cornices above and their vast plate-glass windows below, the breadth of the side-walks and carriage-way, the purposeful prosperous crowds give an impression of size, solidity and dynamic wealth such as I have never experienced in Europe.

I well recall how stimulating I found it all, especially as I walked back to my hotel in the gloaming — the sunset, the lighted windows, the dry, polished street, the keen, clear air. That night, after dinner, I explored some of the lower parts of the town, as one could then safely do. Again I was struck by the contrast between the sleekness of Fifth Avenue and the unkemptness of the ill-paved streets that lay off it. Porter told me it was all due to Tammany Hall being in power. "Streets don't vote: Tammany supporters don't drive: so why waste money on streets?"

When Porter had made all the contacts he wanted, taking me with him everywhere, which I appreciated, we set off one morning for Washington. We did not arrive together. Porter gave unexpected birth to a message to *The Times* on the ferry crossing the North River (the Pennsylvania Station and its tunnel were still under construction) and told me to take it to the telegraph office in Jersey City. Having done so, I deliberately missed the train. I wanted to enjoy quietly my first sight of America. I was disappointed with what I saw: "Journey uninteresting. Country untidy and brown, hinting occasionally at past beauties in the way of autumn tints. But most of it resembles the outskirts of a large town and looks as if the builders had only allowed it to remain on sufferance. Chesapeake Bay, though, pretty and a good sunset."

At Washington, I put up at the Ebbitt House, which used to stand on 14th Street opposite the New Willard. All I remember of the first evening is my surprise at the soft sooty hands that served me at dinner. I was to see many such hands and soon began to like some of their owners. A third of Washington was already colored. But there was no noticeable racism in the residential quarter, where each side seemed to know its place and to be contented with it.

The first weeks were strenuous. Porter poured out telegrams, or the drafts of telegrams that he gave to me to put into shape. An office had to be found; some furniture of Porter's fitted into it, and other furniture bought. Porter wanted a conspicuous office; I a quiet one, more in *The Times* tradition. Economy gained me my way, and we took a secluded suite of rooms in an old building, long since demolished, the address of which was 1410 H Street. That settled, Porter returned to New York and left me to move in, assisted by the colored janitor and furniture shifters. It was a dusty, sweaty but cheerful business, and Porter expressed gratification that Eton and Oxford should have stooped to effective manual cooperation with colored people. I had found rooms in a superior boarding house called the Westminster at 17th and Q Streets. It gave me a good breakfast in my sitting room for thirty-five cents. Other meals I took downtown or, when I felt extravagant, at a neighboring apartment house that offered a dollar dinner. I had meals out because I did not want to be too much involved with my fellow boarders. Some of them, nevertheless, I got to know. An inconspicuous member of the House of Representatives allowed me to pick his brains. A general's widow whose experience went back to the Civil War gave me my first impressions of American army life. It seemed hard and isolated as compared with that of the English regimental officer and his family. A mother and daughter from Georgia gave me an insight into the bitterness left by the Civil War in the South.

The news-gathering community of Washington was very kind to the inexperienced Englishman. It was very small indeed as compared to what it is today. Far fewer newspapers were represented. There were no radio or television people, and photographers were less in evidence. I remember only one representative of a periodical — the *Saturday Evening Post.* I regarded him with respect because he was supposed to earn $25,000 a year. Foreign correspondents could be numbered on the fingers of one hand. Only one of them was English. There was no Press Club. Two years were to pass before it was launched. I was an original member and to my great pleasure was made an honorary life member of the National Press Club on the fortieth anniversary of its foundation. I wonder how many of my founding contemporaries survive to enjoy this privilege.

But the absence of a meeting place did not matter. All who counted knew each other, and I soon felt comfortably at home among a group of people enjoying a freedom of familiar access to cabinet ministers and parliamentary leaders that surprised me. The press seemed to be an accepted part of the mechanism of government to a far greater extent than in the Old World. I asked a veteran newspaperman with European experience whether I was imagining this. He said I certainly was not; years before he had reported Gladstone's Midlothian campaign and had never been allowed even to shake the hand of the great man.

My sponsor in this new world of adventure was Phillip Patchin, a member of the New York *Sun* bureau, somehow or other connected with Porter. We hit it off well together and he worked hard to give me my bearings in the official world, so small in those days that the State, War, and Navy Departments fitted comfortably into their old building alongside the White House. Patchin took me to the Capitol, helped me to arrange for a *Times* seat in the press galleries of the two chambers, and introduced me to some of the leading senators. At the White House he made me known to the President's secretary and to the small group of reporters in the minuscule press room where they lurked to waylay visitors. (Neither the White House nor the departments possessed press secretaries in those days, though some departments, notably Agriculture, circulated printed stuff generously.)

My first visit to the State, War, and Navy Departments was a memorable experience. We joined the other reporters and trooped along the gloomy corridors, bursting in upon minor officials and seeking, nearly always with success, more respectful entry to their superiors. Even with the cabinet ministers there was informality.

The three ministers we saw on that occasion were Elihu Root, Secretary of State, William Howard Taft, Secretary of War, and C. J. Bonaparte, Secretary of the Navy. Root and Taft were to be conspicuous in affairs for many years; Bonaparte was of minor importance. But on that day it was he who most impressed me. He was a descendant of Jérôme Bonaparte and Miss Patterson, and it seemed to me the height of romance that a Bonaparte should be in charge of the American navy. I noted that "he was attractive with his strong face, bright, smiling eyes, and pleasant voice and laugh." Soon afterward he moved to the Department of Justice and I never saw much of him. To Root I often ventured alone even in those early days. He was dry in manner but helpful partly out of kindness and partly, no doubt, because he wanted to inculcate *The Times* with a sympathetic understanding of American policy. I never lost touch with him. I recall, for instance, the lecture he gave me on American neutrality in 1914. He was a strong Republican and had little use for President Wilson and he told me that, as the President was one of those liberals who follows rather than leads public opinion, I was quite safe in assuming that American neutrality would stand an almost unlimited amount of buffeting.

The first impression Taft made was of good-natured jovial-
ity. He was dressed for riding: "What do you think of this
leg?" he asked, patting a boot. "Do well for a grand piano,"
said a white-haired reporter of the Hearst press. The secretary's bulky frame shook with laughter.

My star introduction was to the first President Roosevelt:

> Porter took me to see the President this morning. From the little
> hall in the Executive wing of the White House we went into a
> large room partly divided by projecting sides, each with a panel
> which could be slid across to shut off the smaller part where the
> President and his desk are. The larger part is the Cabinet Room
> in the middle of which are the long mahogany table and the chairs
> of the Cabinet members. In this part of the room many people
> were waiting about. Senators, a clergyman, Melville Stone, the
> head of the Associated Press, with whom we talked, and others.
> We had to wait some time and heard Roosevelt's emphatic voice
> through the closed panels. It is of a slightly falsetto tone — the
> voice of a fat man, though its owner is not fat. He is short, sturdy
> and tough.
>
> Roosevelt has wonderful strong eyes, small brown ones. They
> fix one when he talks and the tremendous personality pours out.
> He shows his teeth and gums. He talked to us mostly about the
> iniquities of Maurice Lowe (the other correspondent of an English
> newspaper resident in Washington) who, he says, is a liar and
> quite untrustworthy and wants to make bad blood between the
> United States and England.
>
> It is wonderful how accessible the President seems to be; and
> yet, in reality, he is strictly guarded by his secret service men.

Not long afterward I bearded the President alone. (My diary
does not mention the reason for this visit.) "He was being
shaved by his coloured barber. He was leaning back in his
chair, face covered with lather which was not much whiter
than his teeth. He talked and gesticulated, and the dexterity
with which the barber anticipated his movements was mar-
vellous." Again the Rooseveltian personality poured over me

like an electric emanation. Northcliffe sometimes affected me in the same manner. No one else has: not even Franklin Roosevelt when President. But that may have been because we were intimates in our thirties, and supermen may be difficult to recognize as such by those who have known them young.

Early in the spring of 1907 Porter announced that he was off for the summer to England. He handed me an invitation to attend the opening at Pittsburgh of a sumptuous institute that Andrew Carnegie, the great ironmaster, had presented to the city. I traveled to Pittsburgh on a wet April day and found myself one of several hundred guests from all over the world. The Kaiser sent a personal representative with a charming wife, and a telegram on the day; the French government sent the Director of the Trocadéro; all the principal countries were officially represented, except Great Britain.

Moberly Bell, the most important of the various unofficial English guests, was volubly indignant at this unimaginative ineptitude. I turned his remarks into a message to *The Times* about British official parochialism and bad manners. I showed it to Bell and asked him to add his signature to mine so as to insure that the message was not discarded as irresponsible. This he did. That night, after dinner, he said that the telegram had been a good one. He inquired what I was being paid and found the fifteen pounds a month that I had been given on going to America quite inadequate. "From now on," he said, "you shall have fifty pounds a month."

Not since I had been given my house football colors at school a year before I expected them had I experienced such a sense of triumph. The scene comes vividly back to me: the hotel sitting room with its electric light arrangement of varnished brass in the center of the ceiling, the metal imitation log on the fireplace spouting bluish jets of gas, heavy armchairs, a rocking chair, the rich red carpet and curtains, Mr. and Mrs.

Bell sitting comfortably relaxed, he and I with glasses of port. I dispatched to London Bell's instructions about my salary and told F. that we could marry. To my parents I said nothing. I knew they would think me rashly impetuous, and I could see no use in courting epistolary discord as they were coming over to visit me in the autumn.

We traveled back to New York in the private car that George Westinghouse, of pneumatic brake fame, had lent the Bells. The car was of unbelievable opulence. Its walls were inlaid with rare woods and the dining compartment silver was as rich as the food and wine. In the morning there was no question of our being turned out of the train, like other travelers, onto the chilly decks or into the overheated interior of the ferry across the North River. We were bundled straight into a warmed bus and sat in it until we reached the Belmont Hotel, near Grand Central Station and long since demolished, but then advertised as the newest thing in hotels, with more square yards of looking glass above ground and more floors below ground than any rival possessed. We stayed there as Carnegie's guests. I was not even allowed to pay for braces bought in the barber's shop.

That day the *New York Times* gave Bell a lunch at which all available celebrities were present from Joseph Choate to Mark Twain. Then the Bells sailed home; and I returned to Washington very happy.

I found myself in completely congenial circumstances that summer of 1907. Everybody was kind; everything was interesting and vivid and I was soon to be married.

The most romantic of American Presidents was at the height of his many-sided vigor, and was writing, in graphic language, the first pages in a new and still unfinished chapter of American history. It was all excitingly different from the Old World. There was a sense of change, exploration, and development quite new to me. Bitter controversy, political and social, was

in progress but it was taken for granted that, whatever its results, the country would inevitably go from strength to
strength. In the United States it was spring, a tempestuous
and unsettled spring but invigorating; in Europe it was
autumn with a grim, uncertain winter ahead. Such were the
sort of generalizations I was noting in my diary. I noted, too,
that "we of the press watch the White House as children watch
a conjuror wondering what is next coming out of the hat; but
certain that whatever it may be, it will make news." It might
be a smashing attack on "big business," on "malefactors of
great wealth," on "men with hard faces and soft bodies" upon
whose iniquities "muckrakers" like Upton Sinclair and Ida Tar-
bell were busily dilating, or it might be encouragement to the
President's protégé, the "little man," or advice to mothers
about their families, or a lecture to the nation about not wast-
ing its natural resources. Or somebody might be nominated to
the Ananias club, often a newspaperman who had said the
wrong thing. Some of my colleagues so suffered; it did not
worry them. Membership was usually short. It was said that the
President would occasionally allow a writer to reveal exclu-
sively some project he was meditating with the proviso that,
if the idea failed to catch on, he would be disowned.

Professionally nothing could have been better for me than to
be left on my own after the tonic of Moberly Bell's appreciation.
I felt a full-fledged journalist. My cutting book of those days re-
veals the growth of self-confidence. My telegrams gain substance and variety; articles sent by post begin to appear.

Lists of forgotten or half-forgotten names are no good to anybody, but there are two colleagues who must be mentioned,
for I quickly made working alliances with them, one of which
lasted all my time in America. This was with George Hill,
head of the New York *Tribune* bureau, and the other, Edward
Lowry, correspondent of the New York *Evening Post*. Ed Lowry
was a volatile, brilliant Southerner. He was also a good,

though cynical, judge of politics, about which his convictions were not deep. He was excellent company. George Hill was a stolid Northerner, an earnest Republican, and, therefore, in his element as the correspondent of the principal Republican paper. Everybody trusted him, and he was intimate with the Republican leaders in Congress and outside it, to many of whom he made me known. At first it was one-way traffic as between Hill and Lowry (and to a less but still helpful degree, a few other American colleagues) and myself, for I had everything to gain and nothing to give. Then, as I made friends in the diplomatic world I was gradually able to make some repayment, for relations between the press and the foreign missions were not then close, and the Rooseveltian dynamism was giving a news value to American foreign policy, and to the world's reception of it. Here again I was lucky.

My first reportorial task on our arrival in Washington was to discover why Sir Mortimer Durand, the British Ambassador, was resigning. Durand was resigning because, though a great authority on Asia, he had not been a success in America. I did not, of course, know that at the time, but I emerged reassured from the embassy, having discovered there two seniors whom I knew at home and a member of the chancery who had been in the same house with me at school. The two seniors were Esme Howard, the Counselor (afterward Lord Howard of Penrith), and Ronald Lindsay, the First Secretary, both of whom ended their careers as ambassadors in Washington. With the French Embassy, too, I had a link in the shape of an acquaintanceship between the Ambassador, Jusserand, and my father. With that start and the prestige of *The Times* I was soon on adequate terms with the other Old World missions, and also with the Japanese, which was important because there was tension that summer between America and Japan.

My parents came over in the autumn. Having people like the Russian and Japanese counselors to the modest parties I gave for them (the British and French Embassies had not returned from their summer quarters) helped me to persuade them that I really was doing well enough to marry at once. Persuasion was not easy, but, once it was completed, my father behaved with his usual generosity and promised to arrange things so that, if the worst came to the worst, we should not starve. After Washington, I took my parents down to Old Point Comfort where I had stayed during the spring to report the celebration of the three-hundredth anniversary of John Smith's landing, a very modest affair as compared with the festivities of fifty years later; then via Norfolk up to Richmond and on to New York whence, after seeing the *New York Times* produce itself, which impressed them, they sailed for home, still, I am afraid, somewhat dubious about my prospects.

In due course I followed them across the Atlantic and spent Christmas at home, saw *The Times* people, told them that I was going off to Italy to get married, and asked them to prolong my holiday by another month. This they did. I wondered gratefully at their patience with me. I did not know that *The Times* was then at the supreme crisis of its existence, that the negotiations which were soon to end in Lord Northcliffe's acquisition of control were in hectic and uncertain progress. An inconspicuous member of the staff could not have chosen a better time to play truant.

We were married at Genoa to avoid a conventional wedding. F. was at Alassio with her mother, who was ailing and had been sent south for the winter. We went to Sestri Levante and on to Viareggio, then a small seaside resort and fishing village very different from the Mediterranean Margate it had become when we saw it again thirty years afterward. Then on to Rome and Naples where we boarded the White Star ship *Cedric*.

CHAPTER 4

London Interlude

WE SETTLED DOWN COMFORTABLY in Washington. My Pittsburgh promotion had moved me to desert my boarding house and take a little flat downtown on K Street between 14th and 15th Streets. The flat was quiet, airy in summer and sunny in winter, and it cost only fifty dollars a month. I had furnished it sparsely. F. embellished it. My fat, good-natured colored cook took to her and the food improved. We were welcomed by the friends I had made; new friendships began to be formed; my work went well and after a few months Porter returned to England as he had done the year before. But my clearest memories of this, our first period in America, is not of people, or of my work; it is of Washington, its streets, its surroundings, and its weather.

Washington was still a comparatively small and quiet town. How quiet is shown by the nature of the vehicle which took us to and from parties. It was a funny little buslike contraption, called a herdic, which seated two people comfortably, four uncomfortably. Its door was at the back and it was drawn by a single horse — usually an old and slow one. On arrival it pulled out across the street, backed up to the curb, and decanted its passengers. It was not to last much longer; it belonged to empty streets, to what Franklin Roosevelt called the "horse and buggy age." The motorcar was coming in; Washington was growing; the apparatus of government, though still microscopic compared to what it is now, was increasing and the town was becoming each year a more fashionable pleasure center. One could see the process going on — palaces interspersed by Negro shacks, streets paved and named but lacking houses. Massachusetts Avenue ran into the open country a few hundred yards beyond Sheridan Circle. There was only a small group of houses beyond the Connecticut Avenue bridge and then nothing much till Chevy Chase. There were no outer suburbs; Alexandria was an unregarded relic of Colonial days; Georgetown the haunt of Negroes with a few cheap apartment houses for government clerks. Great Falls and even Little Falls were in deep country. Arlington and Fort Myer lurked among fields and woods; Potomac Park was partly swamp and the Lincoln Memorial did not exist; Mount Vernon could only be reached with comfort by steamer.

We reveled in the accessibility of the country. In the spring and autumn, that is to say. The summer was too hot and the winter too cold to make country walking a staple exercise.

My first excursion into the West took me to the 1908 Democratic Convention at Denver. George Hill chaperoned me. He and his colleagues found it dull. The nomination of W. J. Bryan, the great radical leader of the Middle West, was as inevitable as his ultimate defeat by William Howard Taft whom Theodore Roosevelt had named as his successor. To me the meeting was fascinating. At first I was dazed by its ritual, by the marching and countermarching, the waving of flags, the blaring of bands, the oratory, the intrigues, the bargaining, and the rumors. Then it was borne in on me that behind the ballyhoo there was much practical sense, that the national conventions were not only effective machines for the choosing of candidates but, what was equally important in those days when radio and television were unknown, also for the fusing of continentwide parties into workable wholes. They gave local leaders the opportunity of seeing, hearing, and even conversing with the men at the top and sent them away feeling that they had a share in the selection of candidates. Inversely it gave the men at the top the opportunity of impressing themselves upon the mob and of learning how its members were reacting to them. The diversity of the types upon the floor of the hall stressed the need for this mechanism — paunchy, townbred Eastern "bosses"; ponderous politicians from the South with their frock coats, shoestring ties, and black sombreros; lean and sun-tanned delegates from the Desert States; Bryan's effervescent followers from the Middle West, believers in free silver, fundamentalism, and the kinship of Wall Street and the railways with the Powers of Darkness.

I was glued to the window during the daytime on the journey out. One crossed mountains, limitless farmlands, great rivers; climbed gradually upward over more or less open prairies until the Rocky Mountains rose over the curve of the globe; and reached Denver 6000 feet above the sea. But I still was not much more than halfway across the continent. I returned to Washington with a more serviceable appreciation of the American scale of distances than I had been able to obtain from maps, books, or conversation.

Denver disappointed me. The more I learned of the United States, the more fascinated I had become by the telescoping of history, by the closeness of a different past to the actual present. In England my parents had only known the smug placidity of Victorian progress. In the United States in the course of the same short period great events had occurred swiftly, dramatically, and violently. The Civil War had been fought, vast

railways built, the West tamed and colonized, the Indians conquered, the buffalo exterminated. Many of the older men I
was getting to know had fought in the war between the states
on one side or the other. Negroes not much above middle
age would tell one that they had started life as slaves. On the
battlefield of Gettysburg small cannonballs were visible in
the trunks of trees as though embedded yesterday. But Denver was just a large, well-planned modern city with broad
streets, handsome buildings, and a normal bustling population. There was nothing of the Wild West about it.

Back in Washington aviation was added to the subjects about
which I had to report. The Wright brothers were rumored to
be doing well with their heavier-than-air machine; another
such project was in progress in California; and more than one
lighter-than-air machine had left the ground. There was keen
controversy between supporters of the two types. The War
Department inclined at first to favor lighter-than-air machines,
and plans were even drafted for an Aerial Defense Navy. Alex-
ander Graham Bell, the Scottish-born scientist who invented
the telephone, took the other side, and in the library of his
house on Connecticut Avenue, he gave me most of the information upon which my articles and telegrams were based. He
was certain that practical flying was on its way.

Excitement stimulated controversy when it was learned
that the Wright brothers were ready to have their machine officially tested above the parade ground at Fort Myer, the military station in Virginia just across the Potomac. Orville Wright
made several unofficial preliminary flights. On the evening of
the official test F. and I drove out and joined the group of
watchers on the parade ground, but before the flight I went
off alone to the far end of the ground so as to get the best possible view. Orville Wright with a passenger, Lieutenant Selfridge of the American army, lifted the machine into the air.

It resembled a large box kite and labored noisily several times around the field. Then on turning the corner nearest to me it lost its balance and momentum, like a bird killed on the wing, and crashed to the ground from a height of about 100 feet. Wright had broken bones, Selfridge's skull was fatally fractured.

That was on September 17, 1908, and I wonder whether I may not have the gloomy distinction of being the first person to try to rescue the first airplane fatality in history. Yet it was not the crash that I recalled most vividly afterward, but the tense silence of the other spectators as they ran toward the wreck, and then my rush back to town on a borrowed bicycle to scribble at the telegraph office a nice little "scoop."

Meantime a dull presidential campaign led up to Election Day, the results of which Porter, not long back from England, dealt with from New York. I stayed in Washington and was glad I did so, for on the day after Taft's election, President Roosevelt held an embryo news conference — I suppose there were about twenty of us present and no women. The President was bubbling over with satisfaction. "I said a few days ago that we should beat the Democrats to a frazzle." "What," somebody asked, "is a frazzle?" "A frazzle is a good Southern word; and, if people want to know its significance, the election returns should enlighten them."

No President can have left office more happily. His chosen successor was coming in to carry out a program that he had defined and for which he thought he had cleared the way. A little later on he and Mrs. Roosevelt gave a ball at the White House. It was a good ball. "Everybody" was there. This meant that the majority of the guests, being satisfied with the world as it was, were critical of the radicalism of their host. F.'s diary records that when somebody alluded to this, Roosevelt replied: "Let them talk. They think they can attack me because I am the setting sun. They forget that the whole sky can be filled with the effulgence of the setting sun." And again: "If only I could have had a baby born in the White House, my cup would have been full."

Soon after the election Porter appeared in Washington (he preferred to spend his time in New York) and announced that Printing House Square wanted me back in London. He said they were satisfied with my work, but Washington was increasing in importance and they thought it well that as many of their young men as possible should know something about it. This blow was not lightened when Hill and other friends averred that the real reason for my being shifted was that Porter thought I was beginning to cut more ice in Washington than he could hope to do. They pointed out that Porter, as an old Republican hack, was a back number, that neither Roosevelt nor Taft had much use for him, nor anybody else so far as they knew. Hill told Cabot Lodge, the chairman of the Foreign Relations Committee of the Senate who had befriended me from the start, about what had happened, and Lodge wrote me a letter to show at home should I find that Porter had been running me down. He wrote that he had heard with great regret that I was no longer to be *"The Times* correspondent here"* and that "your relations with that part of the Government with which I happen to be connected have been most agreeable," and he stressed the importance of *The Times* being well represented in Washington.

We embarked for home in February 1909. We left our furniture in Washington and a year later almost to the day, I was back there in Porter's place.

We landed at Liverpool and traveled south in winter sunshine through snow-covered country. As we entered London the sun became obscured by fog, and we emerged from the station into drab streets smelling of coal smoke, gin, tobacco, and stale beer in a miserable four-wheeler rattling along on its iron tires. Behind trotted one of the tattered cab runners who hung about stations and followed four-wheeler cabs in the hopes of a tip for unloading the luggage.

In the West End, the air was cleaner and the smell of the moldy straw on the floor of our conveyance oozed up to replace the miasma of the meaner streets. Our lodgings in Kensington were dilapidated, gloomy, and cold. Even F. was daunted by the grimness of it all, and I was uneasy about my reception at Printing House Square. Lavino was dead. Had he been alive I should have been confident that in Paris or elsewhere he would find me a job. I still had Moberly Bell, but Northcliffe now controlled *The Times* and our first meeting in Washington a few months before had been inauspicious. I had not liked him, and years afterward, when I liked him very much indeed, he told me that I had been right in feeling that he on his side had thought poorly of me.

Next day the depression lifted. My reception at Printing House Square was friendly and a place awaited me in the Foreign Department with the same salary I had been receiving in America, which was generous considering how much cheaper it was to live in England. No objection was raised to my writing articles for the New York *Evening Post* as it had asked me to do. Indeed they seemed to be impressed that so responsible a newspaper was prepared to depend on me for its London stuff. On my return to Kensington I found that the domestic situation had also brightened. My mother-in-law had put her comfortable little house in Campden Hill Road at our disposal for an indefinite period, as she preferred Scotland.

Almost my first task at the office was to write the leading article on President Taft's inauguration. It was all wrong. It prophesied success for the new President. But that did not matter, as everybody expected the same, and it gave me a good start. After that I worked away contentedly. I subedited, wrote one or two leading articles, did paragraphs and a special article occasionally, coming to the office about teatime and leaving soon after midnight.

By day I wrote my pieces for the *Evening Post.* It was a good year during which to contribute articles from England to a serious American newspaper. The German menace was making news; the big navy people were agitating; conscription was in the air. Domestic politics were spectacular. The balance of society was teetering. Lloyd George helped by Winston Churchill was laying the first foundations of the welfare state; the House of Lords was threatened with the loss of its constitutional teeth if it interfered on behalf of outraged privilege. The bitterness was extreme, worse than that in America over Theodore Roosevelt's progressivism. Obvious comparisons could be made, but not carried too far, as the Lloyd George program was thought to be to socialism and the Rooseveltian only meant a reformed capitalism. I wrote lighter articles about things that were vanishing or doomed to vanish: about cab runners, crossing sweepers, foot warmers in railway carriages, and other things odd to Americans, the Lord Chamberlain's censorship of plays that Bernard Shaw was brilliantly attacking, the Eisteddfod, suffragettes, university reform. I wrote about nationalism in India and Egypt, about the new South African Union and the color question there, about horse breeding, divorce, and the Thames.

At Printing House Square the Northcliffian infiltration was in full process. A few days after my arrival the staff gave the editor and his assistant, Capper, a dinner to celebrate the twenty-fifth anniversary of their appointments. Of the seventy of us present only two were Northcliffe men, the chief printer and the advertisement manager. There was a similar dinner three

months later of which the seating plan has also survived. I
think it must have been given by Northcliffe. Anyhow there
were plenty of his people at it. Northcliffe presided with Buckle
on his right and Moberly Bell on his left; Bell was hemmed in
on his other side by Lord Rothermere, the ablest of Northcliffe's
brothers, and Buckle by Kennedy Jones, a tough, dominating
type from the *Daily Mail* who used to hint that Northcliffe owed
him more than people realized. I sat at the humble end of a
lower table and had as neighbors Northcliffe's private secretary
and Reginald Nicholson, Northcliffe's chief man on the staff of
The Times and soon to be its manager. He was quiet, imperturbable, and efficient, an excellent shock absorber between
the old and the new.

The atmosphere of Printing House Square was heavy with
apprehension, resentment, and suspicion. I seem to remember that blinds would be pulled down for fear that eyes on
one side of the square should espy some conclave on the other.
Northcliffe's minions prowled about. They were pleasant
and tactful and were at first mainly concerned with the business arrangements of the office. But the editorial side knew that
its turn would come and feared for its personnel and policies.
Northcliffe used to send us a frequent sheet of terse criticism or praise. It was known as the X, the symbol that Northcliffe, who was addicted to melodramatic mystery, had adopted
during the early months when his proprietorship was supposed
to be secret. But it never occurred to me at the time that its
significance was anything but pejorative — short for excre-
ment. Again my luck held. The Foreign Department and its
expenses were investigated not, like the others, by people
from the Harmsworth organization but by a member of the Walter family in the person of Ralph, one of Arthur Walter's nu-
merous half brothers. He used me as his assistant, and this
association developed into a close friendship valuable to me

then and afterward. It taught me more about the current
strains and anxieties than my situation entitled me to know.
Moberly Bell was under the heaviest pressure. He wilted so
visibly that we called him the "Weary Titan." Northcliffe that
autumn told him he needed a change and took him to America,
but the trip did not help him as there were constant parties
and endless discussions of the problems of *The Times*. But it
helped me enormously. Bell came back confirmed in what
was the mounting opinion of the office that Porter was not the
man for Washington. Nor did he consider that Hargrove, the
assistant who had succeeded me, was fit for Porter's shoes. He
asked me to return there as chief correspondent. Bell said that
he had heard satisfactory things of F. and myself while in America, and that Chirol spoke well of me, and especially of a long
article upon American politics that I had recently concocted
with the help of the managing editor of the New York *Evening
Post*, who happened to be in London.

Within a month or so I was off to America again, glad to be
well away from Printing House Square and sorry for its inhabitants among whom I felt I had established new relationships
both serviceable and agreeable. Bell, Buckle, Chirol, Flanagan, and Scott I had known before but the two people with
whom I was to have most to do at first in Washington had not
been in the office during my former sojourn there. They
were D. D. Braham and Edward Grigg (afterward Lord Al-
trincham). Braham had just been summoned from Constantinople to be assistant foreign editor and he succeeded Chirol
as foreign editor, when in 1912 Chirol and Northcliffe became
too much for each other. He was dislodged in his turn by a
Northcliffian explosion two years later and blown out to Australia to be editor of the Sydney *Daily Telegraph*. He was an
able and earnest man to whom fortune might have been
kinder. To me he was most sympathetic, personally and po-

litically. He had been in the Berlin office and was sound on Germany. Before Constantinople he had been the Saint Petersburg correspondent but was too liberal for the tsarist government and was forced to leave.

Edward Grigg had little in common with Braham save that they had both been at Oxford, at New College. Braham was a recluse and lived at Penge and only saw those whom his duties demanded him to see. Grigg mixed energetically with the great world and would come into our room full of the sayings of cabinet ministers. He was an ardent imperialist; it was he, I think, who caused the change of the title of the foreign page of *The Times* from "Colonial and Foreign" to "Imperial and Foreign" as it remained for many years. He had a varied career in front of him as journalist, soldier, courtier, secretary to a prime minister, politician, and proconsul, and our lives were often to touch.

CHAPTER 5

The Times——American Correspondent

I CROSSED the Atlantic ahead of F., baby, and nurse in order to have quarters ready for them in Washington. I landed in a state of blended exhilaration and diffidence. Hargrove, who was returning to London to take my place there, received me with a generosity that has a high place in my collection of good memories. He offered to stay on for a few weeks with me in Washington until I had settled down. The offer, ratified by London, was gratefully accepted. So, after persuading the *New York Times* to find employment for the pathetic little cockney clerk whom Porter had brought out and left behind, I boarded a southbound train.

In Washington a married member of the embassy staff was just going on leave and let me have his house for a month, which, as F. was soon due with our son, Paul, who had been born in London, would give us ample time to find a dwelling place, get our furniture out of storage, and so on. In those days accommodation at short notice was no problem in Washington and I found a flat with the help of the English colony, which, so far as we ever discovered, then consisted, save for a few British-born Americans or American-married Englishwomen, of one man — Harry Wardman.

Wardman, the imprint of whose building activities must still be visible, was a bright-eyed, alert little Lancastrian, dapper and prosperous and fond of boasting that it was only a few years since he had passed through Ellis Island as an immigrant with no other capital than his bag of tools. The latest and best of his buildings was the Dresden, an apartment house at the top of the Connecticut Avenue hill. There we spent a year before moving into a small house on Massachusetts Avenue just beyond Sheridan Circle where we stayed until our return to England.

Hargrove left soon after we had settled in and the process of my making good started. I had by then seen most of my old friends from President Taft downward and had discovered that it would be my fault if I did not succeed. Washington was a newspaperman's paradise that spring. Everything was going wrong; most things were uncertain. The Republican Party, which had dominated affairs since the Civil War, was falling apart. Its conservative leaders who controlled Congress had overreached themselves by forcing through a reactionary high tariff bill and persuading the President to accept it. Its radical elements, the Insurgents, considered the bill a betrayal of the Rooseveltian program. And behind the upheaval loomed the ex-President himself just emerging from the African jungle where he had been pursuing big game. Would he attempt to close the gap in his party or attack Taft, divide his party, and perhaps let the Democrats step into power at the next election?

The external situation offered me other opportunities. The United States was in controversy with us over details connected with the "Open Door" policy in China, which we both favored; the New American tariff law was bringing on important negotiations with Canada; American comment upon our own turgid politics needed attention. I made up my mind that what my output lacked in quality should be made up by quantity. I poured out a stream of telegrams and mailed articles. I worked like a dog and my diligence was rewarded. My salary was raised; my efforts were commended; I was urged to work less hard. At Christmas came a note from Northcliffe and, at the bottom of it, scrawled across the paper in his diagonal script: "You are doing good work."

Next spring I went home for a short visit, during which I learned to know Northcliffe better and met for the first time the other man with whom I was to be most closely in contact at Printing House Square during the coming years. This was Geoffrey Robinson.

Geoffrey Robinson (who a little later altered his name to Dawson, as I shall henceforth call him) had abandoned the editorship of the Johannesburg *Star* to come into Printing House Square in an indeterminate capacity but obviously as Northcliffe's choice to succeed Buckle as editor, as he did the following year. Everybody welcomed his presence. For Buckle it was a relief to know that his successor would be, like himself, a fellow of All Souls. Already that spring Dawson dominated the editorial side of the office, and it was to him I took my problems. That was the start of a wonderfully good alliance between editor and correspondent. I had every reason to be grateful to the "old Gang" and to Grigg and Braham, but they were all soon to go (Moberly Bell, that gallant fighter, had already dropped over his desk, killed by fatigue), but Dawson more than made up for these losses.

The war was not far off, and in it America would at least play a decisive part as the chief source of supply from abroad for the side that controlled the seas. Dawson had never been to the United States, but he was very much of the English-speaking world and understood the problems that a European war would inflict upon Washington. This meant everything to me in the difficult years ahead. I recall thinking how lucky I had been when in Berlin in 1935 the correspondent of *The Times* complained of the way in which Printing House Square, or rather Dawson, ignored his warnings and cut his dispatches. There were, indeed, two Dawsons — the young, alert editor of the First War and the elderly and complacent editor of the Second War, so ignorant of the realities of Europe that he aligned himself with Neville Chamberlain and the appeasers.

Dawson never disagreed with me basically about our treatment of American affairs. Telegrams might be cut down, but their sense was never tampered with. My advice, sometimes volunteered, often asked for, was usually taken. Only over Ireland did we differ. Dawson was for union, I for home rule. Most Americans were home rulers, and not only the Irish Americans. This I used to stress with what tact I could. Dawson nearly always published what I sent and this difference of opinion made no dent in our relationship. Telegraphic instructions and queries were kept down to a minimum. There was no nagging and always patience if one complained or nagged oneself. If someone praised one's work, the remark was passed on, as were criticisms for what, Dawson would deprecatingly write, they were worth. More than once, he was nice about me to somebody who might be expected to repeat to me what he had said. I have a letter from my mother reporting praise of me when she had happened to sit next to him at dinner. Like Northcliffe, he was generous with telegrams of congratulation and thanks. On my visits home he used to take me under his wing, and I have many good memories of his little house in Smith Square (during his first term of editorship he was a bachelor), of walks, talks, and meals together, and of the notabilities to whom he introduced me.

Northcliffe has been credited with having rescued *The Times* from disaster without damage to its essential qualities.

I doubt whether he could have achieved this feat had he not had the sagacity to choose Dawson to help him. My glimpse of both men at work left me with the impression that if Northcliffe saved the body, Dawson saved the soul. Certainly none of the other people then in Printing House Square could have coped with Northcliffe so effectively. Dawson had all the imperturbable toughness expected of a Yorkshire man. He knew when to accept Northcliffe's often irritating interferences and when to resist them. He respected much in Northcliffe and Northcliffe respected much in him. In training, character, and associations the two men were as different as oil and vinegar, but, as with oil and vinegar, their inability to coalesce did not prevent their temporary cooperation for an essential end. Finally each lost patience with the other, but not until *The Times* was strong enough to survive the unsatisfactory period between Dawson's resignation in 1919 and his reinstatement in 1922 after the death of Northcliffe.

Only in Dawson's room in that spring of 1911 was there confidence and decision. Elsewhere the sense of insecurity was even worse than the year before.

Even in America the tension could make itself felt. This was so in the case of the foundering of the White Star liner *Titanic* in the spring of 1912, which gave me the biggest and most sensational bout of reporting I ever had. I rushed to New York on the first vague reports that the great ship, the sister of the *Olympic* whose maiden voyage I had described for *The Times* the year before, had been sunk by hitting ice on her first crossing of the Atlantic.

For two days, as the *Carpathia* carrying survivors from the *Titanic* approached New York, it was necessary to sift into some sense rumors, probable and improbable, wild speculation, and comparatively few indubitable facts. Two telegrams of formidable length resulted. Then after the *Carpathia* had docked came the longest I ever wrote filling some four of the fat five-a-page columns of *The Times* of those days, and it was followed by several others almost as long. I had, to help me, our financial correspondent, our collector of advertisements, and the news service of the New York *World* with which *The Times* then had a connection. I recall particularly the day the survivors landed. Firsthand facts were now available if they could be separated from the blinding chaff of imaginative hysteria that was flying about. Survivors had to be met on the dock or tracked to hotels, and one or two of the right sort captured and guarded from competitors, and I must have received from London more queries and requests during those days than in the course of the whole year. I left the legwork to my helpers, and my memory of it all is of sitting at a desk hour after hour, subsisting on sandwiches, bananas, and coffee, surrounded by newspapers and news slips, receiving telephone messages, interviewing my colleagues and their captives, and getting off my telegram, section after section, against time.

The editorial side of *The Times* cabled congratulatory thanks. But from Northcliffe's manager came a letter that I have lost but that, judging from my reply, must have complained of my missing things and being slow.

In the placid prewar years the tragedy shook the world and posed prickly questions. The *Titanic* had been warned that ice was about. Why, then, did she run at speed through the darkness and strike a floe? How came it that the unsinkable had been sunk? Apparently there were not boats enough to accommodate everybody; was that the fault of the Board of Trade, or the White Star Company, or both? There were ugly stories that the crew lacked discipline, were untrained for the emergency. Were such stories true? A Senate committee hurried to New York for a preliminary inquiry. It prevented the White Star from hustling the surviving officers and crew back to England, some of whom, together with high officials of the company, were cross-examined when the committee returned to Washington. Its eventual report had its points. But the hearings suffered from the ignorance of the sea under which its members, and notably its chairman, Senator Smith, labored. "Had the vessel watertight compartments?" "Yes," said the officer being examined. "Why then did not the passengers take refuge in them?" After that Senator Smith was known as "Watertight Compartment Smith." This was the worst example of lapses that caused criticism in the United States and resentment in England and embarrassed me in my efforts to combine adequate reporting with a minimum of provocation.

The *Titanic* hearings also irked me at a time when I was fully occupied in other directions. That embarrassment proved, however, to be for my lasting advantage, as it caused me to turn to F. for assistance. She sat in at the hearings and, under the tutelage of George Hill, was soon giving me the material I needed. After that she often lent me a hand in times of pressure. She was the most devoted of mothers, but I recall an urgent morning at the office when the telephone rang to tell us that our son Paul had broken his arm. When she was reassured about the doctor being on his way, she went on with what she was doing and was rewarded by a second message that the fracture was of the simplest nature.

Various assistants were sent out to me during my time in Washington. None of them settled down. It may have been my fault. All I know is that good secretarial assistance, my close alliance with George Hill, and the friendship of the other chief American correspondents gave me all the professional help I needed. Also, as I shall be showing, I had during my most difficult years in Washington invaluable help at our embassy.

Lord Bryce was our ambassador during my first years in America. He succeeded Sir Mortimer Durand in 1907 and stayed for six years. He arrived with a portentous reputation. He had written a famous book while still an undergraduate; he had entered Parliament and held office; his *American Commonwealth* was the standard study of the United States, in which he had traveled far and wide and had collected many friends. For an old man his energy was terrific. He dined out vigorously sometimes at unexpected tables. He impressed by his erudition and flattered by his curiosity. He was a familiar sight in the streets of the capital, with his ragged beard, shaggy eyebrows, and untidy dress, walking with eager speed. At church he was ushered as a matter of course into the pew Lincoln had occupied. "This is the British Embassy; there through the window you can see Ambassador Bryce — him with the white beard." Thus would shout the man with the megaphone to the tourists in their "rubberneck" car as it proceeded up Connecticut Avenue past the old British Embassy. Bryce was even the target for a lunatic. But the missile was only a brick and only the window of his study suffered.

The ambassador traveled widely making speeches, lecturing at universities and colleges, basking in the respect accorded to one who was considered to be the greatest academic figure in the Old World. He paid visits to Canada and spent some months in South America, publishing a book about it while still ambassador. This was criticized by his professional colleagues but did nothing to diminish his popular prestige. As a peripatetic advertisement for the United Kingdom he was unequaled. As a diplomat he was less happy. He failed to attain intimacy with the presidents to whom he was accredited. Theodore Roosevelt did not want him. He wanted Cecil Spring-Rice. Spring-Rice had been in Washington before as a secretary of embassy when his brilliant charm had made him a

valued member of a distinguished group to which Henry
Adams, Cabot Lodge, and John Hay, formerly Lincoln's secretary and afterward secretary of state, and Theodore Roosevelt
lent luster. But London thought Spring-Rice too young.

This was a pity. Theodore Roosevelt was in the prime of life
and relaxed as furiously as he worked. He rode, walked, ran,
scrambled up and down rocks, played tennis. His companions
in these pastimes were called the "Tennis Cabinet" and com-
prised two ambassadors, Jusserand, the French ambassador all
my time in Washington, and Speck von Sternburg, the German.

Bryce, for all his energy, was too old to compete. "He was
advertised as a walker," the President was alleged to have complained, "but he doesn't walk." His first appearance at the
White House had not been altogether happy. When he presented his credentials, the President impulsively brushed aside
the official speech of welcome that his secretary of state handed
to him to read, saying that this was not the time for formalities
and launched into an extemporaneous flow of friendly and rather
incoherent sentences. Bryce listened and then turned to Ronald Lindsay and asked audibly, "What did he say?"

The ambassador was kind to me, but, in the matter of news
and advice, unhelpful. He fended off questions by asking them
and was known among American newspapermen as the "human
question mark." I met him for the first time, just after his arrival, at lunch with the Esme Howards and wrote to F. that he
was charming to me about my father and was surprisingly full
of questions. After Esme Howard left I should indeed have
been out of touch with the embassy had not the chancery contained two signal exceptions to Lavino's generalization that
diplomats mature slowly. The first was George Young; the
second was Lord Eustace Percy, who must have joined the embassy just about when Young left it. No two men could have
been more unlike; the only thing they had in common was that
in different ways they were different from their colleagues.

Young had advanced ideas about publicity as an aid to diplomacy. He considered unnecessary secrecy an occupational disease of his profession. He did not remain long in it. He turned to teaching and writing and stood unsuccessfully for Parliament in the Labour interest.

Eustace Percy was unique among the young British diplomats in America in my time. I think Washington was his first post. Unlike his contemporaries, who were content to do their allotted work and to amuse themselves in the society of the town, he at once set out to explore American life, winning friends everywhere, and afterward had a notable career in the political and academic worlds of England. When he died, Felix Frankfurter, then of the United States Supreme Court, wrote to *The Times* that "not even Bryce had such a variegated collection of American friends." Eustace Percy lived for some time in a bachelor household (of which more presently) composed of rising young Americans. He gave the most incongruous parties and made them "go." One such has remained particularly in my mind. It was for his brother, Lord Percy, afterward Duke of Northumberland, then an ADC at Government House in Ottawa. The other English guests were William Gladstone, grandson of the great Gladstone, one of the many young men of promise soon to be killed by the Germans, F., and myself. The only American was Victor Berger, then a curiosity as the first Socialist member of Congress — and the last in my time. After dinner Berger mounted his tub. "You English here, what are you?" he asked. "Soldier," Lord Percy said. "Landowner," said Gladstone. "Diplomat," said Eustace Percy. "Reporter," said I. "Ah," cried Berger, "so there is one of you who works and whom I can respect." In the embassy Eustace gained a position of precocious authority, and during the war shuttled between London and Washington wielding in Anglo-American affairs, as he did later at the Paris Peace Conference, an influence out of all proportion to his seniority.

While Bryce was ambassador the most tiresome negotiations I had to report concerned the tariff relations of America and Canada and the treatment of shipping in the Panama Canal, then on the point of completion. In neither did he play much of a part. He was cold-shouldered by both sides over the tariff negotiations and muddled the Panama tolls business. The project for a reciprocal reduction of certain American and Canadian duties was President Taft's child. He hoped it might assuage the anger of the Republican Insurgents at the high tariff law. He approached the Canadians directly instead of through the British Embassy, thus breaking precedent, allowing, indeed, the Canadians to take the first step toward the present representation of the Commonwealth countries by their own men in the principal capitals.

The conclusions of these negotiations a year later gave me one of the few bona fide "scoops" of my career. There had been a series of meetings between two Canadian ministers and American officials in Washington. Everybody knew that they were coming to an end. But both sides were, for once, successfully secretive. Chance favored me. The daughter of one of the Canadian ministers asked me at a luncheon party on the critical day where the office of the Pennsylvania Railroad was as she wanted to buy tickets for her father and herself back to Ottawa that night. I extricated myself from the party as quickly as I could and got hold of Hill, and we bluffed our respective official American friends into admitting that the treaty was indeed about to be signed and dug up enough details for Buckle to telegraph a few days later: "Thanks and congratulations for Friday's primeur."

The treaty came to nothing. The Ottawa Parliament rejected it; the Liberal government responsible for it went to the country and was defeated. *The Times* was pleased; Grigg in particular did not want Canada to be pulled into the American orbit more than geography necessitated. Bryce, the English Liberal, was suspected by him and others of having encouraged the Canadian Liberals to run counter to the true interests of the Empire. This was unfair. He was simply left out in the cold.

In regard to the Panama Canal tolls controversy the ambassador was open to serious criticism. He was incredibly unalert. In November 1911 Taft announced publicly that the United States had the right to grant to her ships the free use of the canal when it was opened in 1914. He got around the undertaking that foreign shipping should not be discriminated against, contained in the Hay-Pauncefote Treaty, by the doubtful argument that reimbursement by the American treasury to American shipping of the dues it paid would not involve discrimination as it would be open to other governments to do the same for their ships. London allowed eight months to pass before it protested and suggested arbitration. By then it was too late. The President had at last won the temporary applause of the Western radicals, who saw that a free passage for American ships through the canal would be a shrewd blow to the hated railroads. Shipowners on both coasts were equally delighted, and the public felt that American vessels ought to be allowed the free benefit of a great American achievement. This was not the English view. I went home in the summer of 1912 and found indignant surprise that so good a lawyer as President Taft should have taken so doubtful a stand. Canada and the other dominions were equally upset.

The President, worried by the outcry, gave George Hill, who was standing in for me while I was away, a statement for publication in *The Times* that he hoped would reduce indignation. It had no such effect, and I was hardly back in Washington before I was summoned to the hot-weather White House in New England. I found the President annoyed as well as worried. Bryce had been to see him shortly before to suggest arbitration. Mr. Taft answered that he would gladly have accepted arbitration eight months earlier but that now public opinion would not allow it.

The President said that he could not understand how a man so well informed about America and so influential in London could have allowed things to drift as the ambassador had done. He then turned to a possible way out of the impasse. I put the gist of his suggestion into a telegram and returned to Washington feeling that the President had cause for grievance. His good intentions came to nothing. Congress put a clause into the Panama Canal Act giving free passage to American ships, a provision the repeal of which it was left to Woodrow Wilson to bring about by clever argument and pertinacity.

CHAPTER 6

Woodrow Wilson and the Democrats

S IX MONTHS LATER, in the spring of 1913, Lord Bryce retired and Sir Cecil Spring-Rice succeeded him, being now on the wrong side of fifty and therefore, in the estimation of London, at last fit for a post that the greatest of his predecessors (Lord Lyons at the time of the Civil War) had occupied in his forties. His appointment had been announced some months earlier in a manner that nearly caused me to look like a fool. Bryce told me one Friday what was in the wind. The news, he said, must not be published as Spring-Rice had still to be officially accepted as his successor. I might, however, warn *The Times* privately (i.e. give the editor time to prepare a valedictory leading article on him). The ambassador added that he was also telling my competitor of the *Morning Post,* Maurice Lowe. I inquired of the White House when the news could be used; they said not before Monday. So I sent a private message to London, prepared my dispatch for Monday, and put the matter out of my mind. Luck, however, intervened and I was afforded another proof of how profitable it can be for correspondents to frequent drawing rooms.

A great time and place for the exchange of gossip in those days were Sunday afternoons and the house of the Misses Pat-

ton. They were three sisters of Irish extraction whose interest
in affairs was only equaled by their hospitality. "So your ambassador is leaving and 'Springy' takes his place," said one of
our hostesses on that particular Sunday. "How do you know
that?" I asked. "Why, Maurice Lowe," she replied, "he has
just left." I also left, precipitately, for it was obvious that my
Morning Post competitor would not have been using the news
as a social asset had he not already telegraphed it to his paper.
I telephoned to the White House and it was agreed that I
could send my prepared dispatch. The incident did *The Times*
no real harm as I caught the main edition, and it did Lowe no
good.

A few weeks before Spring-Rice arrived I received this characteristic letter from him:

> A long time ago I remember writing at your Father's request
> about you, and now I hope to find you in Washington. I have
> greatly profited already by your telegrams which have invariably
> proved right, and I hope to profit by your counsel. Your mother
> tells me that her first acquaintance with my family was through
> my brother Bernard, who emptied his bath out of a window upon
> her as she was walking beneath it. But I hope you won't avenge
> the injury upon me.

My father must have asked Spring-Rice to back me when
there was talk of my trying to become a diplomat. The bath
incident happened when my parents were staying with H. E.
Luxmoore, the famous Eton master of Victorian days, and
when Bernard Spring-Rice was a boy in his house. Pleasure at
the new ambassador's arrival was enhanced by his being accompanied by his cousin, Tom Spring-Rice (afterward Lord
Monteagle). Tom and I had been at school and college together, his parents and mine were friends, and he and my
mother had been drawn together by their addiction to the
piano.

Thus began four years of as happy a relationship between ambassador and newspaper correspondent as can ever have existed. I no longer, as in Bryce's time, entered the ambassadorial study as a reporter who had to be tolerated as the representative of a powerful but not altogether sympathetic newspaper. I now did so as a friend and collaborator. The dispatches and letters I sent home during the labyrinthine controversies that strained Anglo-American relations while America was neutral in the First War could never have been written without the help of the ambassador's knowledge of international law and the apperceptive speed with which he unraveled the essential from the unessential. I can see him now, sitting at his desk dispensing wisdom seasoned with sardonic wit, a neat, compact figure, gray suit, pale face, short grizzled beard, keen kindly eyes behind steel-rimmed spectacles, a dispatch box or two before him; or standing before the fireplace fingering on the mantelpiece, as likely as not, a little bronze plowshare, one of a batch that William Jennings Bryan, the first of Woodrow Wilson's secretaries of state, had caused to be cast out of the metal of an old gun to commemorate the conclusion of an arbitration treaty with various countries a few weeks after the outbreak of war.

I tried to pay Spring-Rice back by acting as his unofficial press attaché, for in those days embassies had no press officers. I prepared for him, on his arrival and at his request, an analysis of the politics and peculiarities of the leading American newspapers. I brought to see him the journalists he ought to know. Occasionally I would be called on to clear up grievances or misunderstandings between the embassy and journalists. All this I was encouraged to do, just as Eustace Percy was encouraged in his unorthodox way of life, so as to contribute to the mass of often contradictory information by means of which Spring-Rice soon began to chart with uncanny precision the complicated currents of American thought. And I recall the pleasure it gave me when my mother wrote:

> The Master [the Master of Balliol, then Strachan Davidson] has sent me a letter from Cecil Spring Rice [who had been at Balliol] which says: "Do tell Mrs. Willert what an immense comfort and help it is to have her son in Washington. He is a real friend and has been of the greatest use. I don't know what we should do without him."

Ironically, Spring-Rice's arrival coincided with the fall of his Republican friends and the inauguration of Woodrow Wilson as the second Democratic President since the Civil War.

Theodore Roosevelt contributed handsomely to Woodrow Wilson's victory in the 1912 election by forming a splinter Republican party of his own. He did so after his rejection by the regular Republican Convention in favor of the candidacy of President Taft. The Republican quarrel was bitter and rather awkward for me. I had good friends in both camps. President Taft had been extremely kind to me. I still treasure a letter from George Hill on tour with him in the West saying that the ears of F. and myself must have tingled when our names had come up in conversation on the presidential train. On the other hand the bent of my politics was liberal and some of our closest friends were among Roosevelt's leading lieutenants. Two of these deserve particular mention.

They were Ruth and Medill McCormick. Medill belonged to the powerful Chicago clan of his name, his younger brother being the famous Colonel Robert McCormick of the Chicago *Tribune*. Ruth's father was Mark Hanna, the Cleveland millionaire who at the turn of the century dominated the Republican Party from the Senate with ruthless ability on behalf of "big business." In spite of, perhaps because of their powerful and opulent backgrounds Ruth and Medill were convinced "progressives." Medill was one of the best educated and most thoughtful men in American politics. A rabid isolationist when there was question of the United States joining the League of Nations, he was not parochial. Like nearly all Americans he resented England's slowness in giving Dublin home rule and was critical of our colonial policy. He knew Europe at firsthand and mixed well with foreigners, speaking good French. His great charm served him well as a link between the West and the East both politically and socially. He told me that what had first revealed to him the breadth of the gulf that separated those two sections of the country was the arrival of two newly made Eastern friends from Yale to stay with him in Chicago without dinner jackets, which they had supposed were unknown out there.

I held Ruth in admiration and affection. Later on she was one of the first women members of the House of Representatives and Medill graduated from that body to the Senate. Both died prematurely. Ruth was not intellectual like her husband nor particularly well educated. But she radiated vitality and was an adept at the chemistry of party-giving. We made many contacts, social and political, at her heterogeneous gatherings.

To Ruth I owe my most vivid memory of the 1912 campaign. A few weeks before the nominating conventions she took us for a weekend to the farm of her brother Dan Hanna in Ohio, with whom Theodore Roosevelt was staying to make a speech at Cleveland, and thus gave us a glimpse of a very great though at that time turbulent and perhaps wrong-headed man leading a forlorn hope for a cause in which he ardently believed against an erstwhile friend in whom he was bitterly disappointed. I went into Cleveland with Hanna to meet the "Colonel." He ignored us on climbing out of the train and hurried forward to the engine to shake hands with the crew. Then on the way back, this colloquy: Hanna: "Colonel, after tea you must come and look at my herd." Roosevelt: "No, I'd

rather not. I have no use for cows except on the dinner table."
An odd attitude, one thought, for the former owner of a Western ranch.

Roosevelt addressed a packed hall in the evening. It was a rough and brilliant performance. I noted at the time that "he said things to the discredit of Taft which were utter misrepresentations; but of the 8,000 people listening there can have been few familiar enough with Washington to realize what he was doing." Afterward at supper somebody congratulated him on his reception. "Barnum and Bailey," he said, his voice rising shrilly. "Pure Barnum and Bailey. It's my past that brings them; not my future — a trap for politicians like myself."

Before the speech, instead of looking at Hanna's cows, Roosevelt made a few impromptu remarks in a nearby village. Somebody asked afterward whether it was not difficult to find things to say on such trivial occasions. "No," he answered, "it's quite easy. Nice things about the children; nasty things about the 'bosses' and so on." Then, with scorn: "Taft, of course, would be quite capable of talking about child-labor to farmers. All I want to do is to stir them up and get them to vote the right way." But his jibes at the President counted for little as compared to the burning sincerity with which he dilated to us in private upon the reforms he desired and his rueful speculation as to whether he had hurt his cause by going too far in certain directions, playing in public, for instance, with the idea that reactionary decisions by the lower courts might be submitted for approval to a popular referendum. He was not sanguine about his chances of returning to the White House. One felt that he was primarily out to smash conservatism and to punish Taft.

There were two Republican Conventions that year at Chicago. We attended both with the McCormicks. Roosevelt nominated himself at the splinter convention. His party was born vociferously, but never grew up.

In between the two Republican Conventions the Democratic Convention had been held at Baltimore and after endless balloting and raucous discussion the reform Democrats did what the radical Republicans had failed to do at Chicago — imposed upon their party their candidate Woodrow Wilson, thus rendering inevitable their victory in the presidential election.

To watch the Democrats settling into office the following March was like assisting at the first scene of a new play of the course of which one had scant foreknowledge and in which the majority of the actors were unknown. The leading character, especially, was an enigma. He was like a man turned actor late in life who, after a single successful appearance on the provincial stage (as reform governor of New Jersey), had suddenly been cast for the principal role in a metropolitan production of the first importance. On one of his last evenings at the White House President Taft entertained a few of his newspaper friends at dinner. Somebody, in the course of what was an intimate and rather sad occasion, asked our host about his successor. "A strange man, a strange man," he replied, and then after a pause, "I can tell you one thing, though. It will be a long time before you people are hobnobbing round the fire again with the President of the United States."

Mr. Taft was right. Woodrow Wilson had a few journalist friends but to most of us, as I soon reported to Dawson, he was cold, distant, and antipathetic. Nonintercourse with the White House did not embarrass me. Many of my Republican friends were still in Congress; the newspaper corps was unchanged; and in the Cabinet two friends appeared. One was W. J. Bryan, the great leader of Western radicalism. Without his support Wilson would not have been nominated and anyhow Wilson meant to be his own secretary of state. Therefore Bryan got the job for which he was totally unfitted.

My other friend in the Cabinet was Franklin Lane, who had helped me in my first Washington days. Lane was a Canadian by birth, which he used to say spared him the uncomfortable prick of presidential aspirations, and a Californian by adoption. He was secretary of the interior, mellow, genial, a good conversationalist, and greedy for argument. I recall an obstinate dispute with him after dinner about the comparative merits of the Senate and the House of Lords. He maintained that the House of Lords was the unrepresentative remnant of a dead past; I that it represented the brains and skills of Britain more generously than the Senate did those of the United States. To settle the argument I presented him with an analysis of the two chambers prepared with the assistance of Eustace Percy that proved my point.

We met the Franklin Roosevelts at the Lanes' house. Franklin was assistant secretary of the navy, a post that Theodore Roosevelt also held on his way up to the presidency. I doubt, however, whether anybody then felt that Franklin would climb so high, though his drive and ability soon stood out. Our houses were close together; Paul, our son, was only a little younger than his eldest son, James, and they became playmates. Eleanor, slim and graceful, cut a good figure on horseback. But I remember her best as a cheerful hostess with a ringing laugh at frequent dinner parties. Our friendship ripened into intimacy. She became godmother to our eldest grandchild. When Hitler's "blitz" was at its worst she cabled that if we wanted to send the child to America, she would look after her for the term of the war. "Me, go to America now, What an idea!" was Wanda's response to the suggestion.

Our first visit to Hyde Park, the Roosevelt house on the Hudson, was early in the war. Our fellow guests were Josephus Daniels, the Secretary of the Navy, and his wife.

The two men were a strangely contrasting team. Daniels was a Southern newspaper proprietor and politician, pacifist, interested, one felt, less in the fighting qualities of the navy than in its morals and ways of life. He made it dry. He preached the fraternization of officers and men. The story went around of his gazing down from on high upon the funnels of a destroyer and expressing surprise that "the darned things were hollow." Roosevelt, on the other hand, was addicted to the sea and was pretty certain that the United States would soon be driven to fight, chafed at the slow inadequacy of the naval preparedness that the President had halfheartedly authorized.

I used to think that Franklin leaned toward the French and away from us. Like many Americans, high and low, like Senator Lodge, for instance, his many British friends did not imply undiluted approval of the British Empire. I recall a certain acidity in his manner when he showed F. and me a silver bowl with a dent on it and said that we might like to know that the dent had been made by "the boot of one of George III's Hessians." He supposed the bowl must have been tarnished to look like pewter; otherwise it would have been looted. When America joined us in the war there was a trace in him of that impatience that the young sometimes evince at what they consider to be the slowness of mind and movement of their elders.

Between the inauguration and the start of the first war President Wilson was brilliantly successful in the domestic field. After a long, intricate debate, about which London was avid for information, he secured the deletion of the discriminatory clause in the Panama tolls law, he imposed tariff reform and currency reform bills upon Congress, and in other ways asserted his liberalism.

In the foreign field, which was Mexico, he did less well. Not long before he entered the White House a general (Huerta) had grabbed the presidency after murdering his predecessor (Madero) and the country was in chaos, to which Washington wanted to apply a remedy considered by London to be impracticable, and London a remedy that Washington considered immoral. London wanted to give Huerta a chance; Washington wanted to find somebody to oust him, which meant civil war. This seemed to us to be a disastrous exercise in democratic liberalism. It cast doubts upon the President's ability as a politician in spite of his success in the domestic field. Anyhow he lacked the tricks of the game. He could not slap backs or put an arm around shoulders. He was aloof and Olympian. The way for his reforms had been prepared by the preachings of Bryan and Theodore Roosevelt. His followers in Congress were malleable, dazed by unaccustomed responsibilities. Here is my description of him to Dawson at the time:

> The President has developed a genius for playing to the gallery and has got the West behind him. He has made for himself the background necessary for the coercion of a majority in Congress, who unused to power, are in mortal terror of being kicked out and always have their ears to the ground . . . Self-willed and secretive to a fault he is at present in the dangerous position of being intoxicated not only with the sense of power but also with the knowledge that his first use of it (the launching of his reform programme) has been wonderfully successful. But he has not yet had his powers of political management seriously tested, for his successes with Congress have been the successes of mob-popularity helped by a keen imagination and a stimulating self-confidence.
>
> Take a forceful Oxford don, convince him that he is an intellectual superman, place him in a thoroughly congenial atmosphere to manage a lot of people whom circumstances make timid, just in the hearing of the plaudits of the mob; add to his make-up a tincture of that cheap-smartness which distinguishes a certain type of private school-master; and you will have some kind of an idea of the President's political personality.

I was tied to Washington in that sweltering summer of 1913. Not only by my *Times* work but also because I was acting there as an outpost for the embassy, which, according to the pre-First War diplomatic custom, was avoiding the heat in the mountains of New England. Letters and telegrams were passed between the Ambassador Eustace Percy, Tom Spring-Rice, and myself. A few of them survive. Could I discover what was likely to be the fate of this or that commodity named in the tariff bill? Was the President really not going to recognize Huerta? It might be useful for me to know that Sir Edward Grey had rejected the German suggestion that the European powers should urge Washington in a joint note to recognize Huerta. Was this or that item in some other bill likely to be adopted? Some of the questions and allusions are now incomprehensible. What, for instance, was the ambassador referring to when he wrote, "Thank you very much for your seasonable and most useful telegram. You will readily understand the view which Grey will take on this matter. An animal bought for breeding purposes is not much use unless *entire*." Then late in September Tom Spring-Rice wrote that the ambassador was ill and must have a complete rest for some time.

Spring-Rice was back in the embassy in the autumn, but not up to much, and such work as was called for at the ambassadorial level was being done informally but effectively by Sir William Tyrrell (Lord Tyrrell of Avon), then Sir Edward Grey's private secretary. Tyrrell, taking advantage of leave due him, had come over to help his convalescing friend and also to observe the new administration, and out of that autumn sprang a close friendship destined to have a major influence on my life. Tyrrell was received by the President and liked him but was struck by what he called his political immaturity.

CHAPTER 7

Contentment and Then War

THE MEXICAN BUSINESS was boiling up. The President and Bryan not only persisted in boycotting Huerta, to the disgust and disquiet of foreigners in Mexico, including American Ambassador Henry Lane Wilson, who resigned and was replaced by John Lind, a Swede from the Middle West inexperienced in diplomacy and ignorant of Latin America, they were also beginning to encourage counterrevolutionary bandits considerably more bloodstained than Huerta.

"Huerta must go," was their watchword. It seemed incredible that an educated liberal, like the President, could be so unrealistic as to expect a Latin American country seething with brigandage to conduct its politics according to Anglo-Saxon rules. But by the beginning of 1914 he was using Carranza, afterward an ungratefully anti-American President, and two bandits, Zapata and Villa, for the dislodgement of the would-be President. Then came the affair of "Benton's body." Benton, a British ranch owner, visited Villa to complain about something and was promptly killed. Spring-Rice, again in reasonable health, was instructed to secure decent treatment for the corpse and to persuade the President and Bryan of the villainy of their protégé. They asked Villa for an explanation. Villa concocted, out of a treatise on civilized warfare sent him by Bryan for his education, the account of a court-martial, which he averred had justifiably led to Benton's execution. During that period, Spring-Rice used to return from his visits to the State Department sparkling with epigrammatic indignation. "The man [Bryan] regards Villa as a sort of Robin Hood sent to impoverish the rich and enrich the poor." "He's like a horrid mass of jellified sentimentality from which a sharp beak occasionally pokes out and snaps." And once when we happened to meet outside the State Department: "Talking to Bryan is like talking to a bad smell." Yet, like nearly everybody who knew him well, he had an affection for Bryan.

Then the Huertistas insulted the American flag: naval detachments were landed at Vera Cruz, lives were lost, hands were wrung in Washington. Then Huerta suddenly quit. But chaos continued, though after August 1914, *The Times* and its readers paid little attention to it.

I enjoyed the Mexican business. Spring-Rice encouraged me to be as downright as I could be in my dispatches. He hoped, vainly, that indignation in London would enable him to persuade Washington to give Huerta a chance. So I tried to bring my messages up to the borderline of sensationalism. I was helped by having spent a few weeks in Mexico soon after the fall of Porfirio Díaz. One of the objects of my visit was to find a local correspondent for *The Times,* and I persuaded an Englishman engaged in business there to undertake the job. Like everyone else in the foreign colony he was horrified by Washington's interference with the normal processes of Latin American revolutionary politics and foreign exploitation but, wishing to play safe so far as his own affairs were concerned, confined himself to occasional objective news telegrams and sent what he would really have liked to say to me by letter, anonymously, to be worked into my dispatches. I was moved by one such communication to say that Huerta's brigand opponents were "inspired by the old Aztec spirit which in pre-Spanish days prompted the priests to cut out the hearts of their living victims" and to give a more than usually depressing account of what was happening beyond the border. "Thanks, congratulations, excellent message heart-surgery," Dawson cabled next day. That was the sort of thing that made being a *Times* correspondent so worthwhile in those days.

I think, indeed, as I look back at it all, that I was more pleased with life during 1913 and the first six months of 1914 than ever before or since. Certainly the year before the First War constituted the most carefree and satisfactory period of my career as a correspondent. The German menace was obscured by events nearer at hand. Dawson's "heart-surgery" telegram was not the only one of the same nature evoked from him by my handling of the Mexican business and of the debates in Congress. Northcliffe, too, contributed in the same manner to the sharpening of my sense of adequacy.

We were happy and lucky, too, in our social relationships. This hospitality of many houses remains gratefully in my mind. In some of them education mingled with social pleasures. This was particularly the case with the bachelor establishment that Felix Frankfurter presided over. He has described it in his delightful dictated reminiscences. It was called the House of Truth and was a small house in an obscure red-brick street with a large room built into the back garden. In that room the company drank, ate, and talked into the small hours of the morning. We were very often there. Felix relates in his book how F. tried in vain to persuade him to bring more method into his housekeeping. But if the housekeeping was haphazard the talk was good. It was predominantly that of questing youth at a time when the country was seething with

problems, social, economic, and political. It opened to me a
window upon the American scene other than those through
which I had been attempting to view it. It was led by Felix,
then in the full vigor of his scintillating youth. Theodore
Roosevelt, we were told, had called him not long before the
most brilliant young man in America.

Most of its participants were liberal or radical in outlook.
Herbert Croly, who founded the *New Republic* after writing
The Promise of American Life, Walter Lippmann, already
known, like Croly, as the precocious author of forward-looking,
thought-provoking books — both of them I probably first met
and learned to like in that back room, with its table at the near
end and its chairs and sofas beyond by the windows.

It was in the House of Truth that Eustace Percy lived for a
time to escape from the diplomatic round and learn about America. All passing visitors thought likely to contribute something were invited to its parties. I recall among them Lowes
Dickinson and Harold Laski as representatives of British radicalism and John Galsworthy of British conservatism. One
of its members was the Canadian, Loring Christie, then I think
doing something for some branch of the American government
but soon to join the Canadian Foreign Service and destined
years later to rise to be his country's ambassador in Washington, where he died. He was well up to the average of the House
of Truth for brains and raised its average for good looks.

There was Aaron Aaronsohn, a Palestinian Jew, an unfor-
gettable figure of romance and energy, fair-haired, blue-eyed,
immensely strong, a formidable boxer, the son of a Rumanian
settler who had prospered. He came to Washington to advise
the Department of Agriculture about the growing of wheat
upon arid soil. He was back in Palestine when the war started
and, being a Turkish subject, was compelled to enlist. His
standing as a scientist won him a commission and he became

scientific adviser to the Turkish army for the projected invasion of Egypt. He pondered upon means of using his position to help the Allies. An invasion of locusts from the direction of Egypt gave him his first chance. He told the staff that there would be no forage for the horses and mules unless the locusts were stopped and said that the first thing to do was to dig trenches against them. Thus he secured information about the tools, transport, and engineering organization of the Turks. Then as the locusts continued, he said that he must go out into the desert toward the Suez Canal and destroy their eggs. He was given a party, selected by himself, and reached the canal, made touch with the British, and returned to the Turks. The locusts stopped in the natural course of events as he knew they would, and his stock was so high that he was ordered to Constantinople to conduct an inquiry into the food situation in Turkey.

Aaronsohn felt that the Allies would also find his report useful. But how was he to get away from the Turks? He returned to his army and his luck was in. There was a shortage of petrol. He told his general that this was a case of dearth among potential plenty, for not far away there were masses of oil shale. The shale was, however, of a peculiar quality and there was only one man in Europe who could deal with it, a difficult character domiciled in Holland. The general ordered Aaronsohn to fetch him. Aaronsohn stayed in Berlin on his way to The Hague and learned things that made him more anxious than ever to reach England. At The Hague the British legation refused to have anything to do with this forceful and mysterious foreigner (*"chinoiserie diplomatique,"* he afterward complained).

Aaronsohn returned to Berlin. There he persuaded the Germans that he could serve the Central Powers better in the United States than in Turkey. He was given false papers and boarded a neutral ship bound for New York. He knew that we should search the ship at Kirkwall and took steps to make sure that he would be taken off in spite of the convincing respectability of his papers. He introduced himself to a girl whom he rightly took to be a minor German agent on her way to the United States, and she gave him some compromising literature, which he left half-hidden in his cabin. The British searchers swallowed the bait and Aaronsohn was removed from the ship protesting violently. Then came what he afterward said was the worst difficulty in the whole adventure, namely persuading "the dolt of a colonel" in command to allow him to telephone to Eustace Percy at the Foreign Office. He was killed eventually in an airplane smash between London and Paris during the Paris Peace conference — a sad loss for Israel.

Another bachelor establishment, as different from the House of Truth as chalk from cheese, gave me a conservative counterbalance to Frankfurter's residence: 1718 H Street, a pleasant, old-fashioned house a door or two from the Metropolitan Club and now replaced by a shapeless utilitarian building. Its frequenters were for the most part conservatives and Republicans, though one of them, Willard Straight, had, together with his wife, found the money to help Herbert Croly launch the *New Republic*. They were soldiers, diplomats, and men of affairs. Only about half a dozen of them lived in the house. The rest of the group came and went. I could generally get a bed there during the hot weather when I had to be in Washington and F. and Paul were at the seaside. The most distinguished member of the group was General Leonard Wood, who commanded Theodore Roosevelt's Rough Riders when the Americans were turning the Spaniards out of Cuba. Afterward he governed Cuba before becoming chief of staff of the army. He was an unsuccessful candidate for the Republican presidential nomination in 1920. Before that, during the 1914 war, he advocated preparedness so vigorously that President Wilson ignored his claims to a high command in the expeditionary force. Wood, being married, did not live at 1718, but he was always in and out of the house.

My relations with friends and informants were not injured by my criticism of the President and Bryan. I had no personal relations with the White House to be injured, and, as for Bryan, he was too hardened a politician to be stung by distant words. He reproached me for my failure to appreciate the high moral purpose of his chief and himself, accused *The Times* of being the cat's-paw of the "finance-Imperialists" of London, New York, and Montreal, and asked us to a dinner at which I expected the lecture to be continued. But it turned out to be a large party to which our invitation was just the impulse of a good-natured man.

As for Bryan's colleagues in the Cabinet, their private opinions of the Mexican foray, like that of the generality of officialdom, resembled quite often those that inspired my writings. Then the 1914 war spoiled everything.

When the Germans smashed into Belgium we were at Marion on Buzzards Bay, a delightful place to which the McCormicks had introduced us. We had taken a small house there so that F. and Paul could escape the southern heat and I enjoy a month's rest after the strenuosities of the Mexican trouble and the Panama tolls debate. It was to be five years before that month's rest was achieved. Washington believed that the Sarajevo crisis would fizzle out like its forerunners. Bernstorff, the German ambassador, sailed for home shortly after the assassinations. We lunched with him and his wife before they left and I cannot remember any serious discussion about them. The British and French ambassadors had already crossed the Atlantic.

I hurried back to Washington, but according to my book of cuttings, I sent nothing to *The Times* for over two weeks. I supposed Northcliffe and Dawson believed that newspaper readers were for the time interested only in the fighting. Among Americans the interest was intense and so was the anxiety as the Germans drove through Belgium. There were of course exceptions, but from the first, sympathy for the Allies, or dislike of Germany, lurked behind the official neutrality of the government, a fact that mitigated very considerably the discomforts of the representatives of the Allies.

But how would the country feel? Most of my time during those waiting weeks was spent upon that question.

The shade of Lafayette still brooded beneficently over Franco-American relations. Officially Anglo-American relations were fairly good. We had been the first of the great powers to recognize the growing importance of the United States by promoting our legation to an embassy some twenty years previously, and since then we had been at pains to foster friendship, sometimes yielding to American claims as in the Alaska-Canadian boundary dispute. But British prestige and mass popularity were low. Ancient prejudices dating from the War of Independence, which in those days the history books often did less than nothing to contradict, had been strengthened by recent events. The South African war had been condemned as a piece of smash-and-grab imperialism. The Irish question was seething, and to most Americans no valid obstacle was discernible to prevent Dublin from being granted home rule. Sympathy with Indian nationalist aspirations was pronounced. The United States had granted independence to Cuba and was preparing to grant it to the Philippines, both of which she had taken from Spain by force of arms a few years earlier.

Nor, as I have said, did Lloyd Georgian radicalism appeal to American individualism. England was felt to be degenerating. The threat by officers to refuse to obey orders to coerce Ulster and the suffragette agitation with its sometimes tragic flouting of the law were regarded as symptoms of this process.

Insensitivity also from time to time marred our official relationship. London's carelessness over the Carnegie celebrations at Pittsburgh was a typical example of this. So was our refusal to take part in the exhibition to be held in San Francisco in 1914 to celebrate the opening of the Panama Canal, a refusal about the ineptitude of which I was allowed to amuse myself by some caustic telegrams to *The Times*. And, as I have shown, the handling of the tolls dispute was also marred by carelessness.

The Germans, on the other hand, had been angling for American popular good will for years with meticulous pertinacity. Their agents pervaded the continent from Canada to Mexico. Peripatetic propagandists from Prince Henry of Prussia downward harped upon the virility of the fatherland and preached to the powerful German-American communities that continued loyalty to the fatherland was not incompatible with the duties of American citizenship. Plans for propaganda were laid, key consulates strengthened. In my own experience the contrast between British drift and German thoroughness was at its most glaring in Mexico City in 1911. I particularly wanted information about the country's economy. Our legation, with its hands full of political problems and understaffed, sent me to the consul. I discovered this functionary, who had spent his life and lost his health in the East, lurking in lonely neglect at the top of a squalid old Spanish building in an office reached by an outside staircase hung with the washing of other tenants. He was useless to me. A day or two later I met von Hintze, the German Minister, and for a short time at the end of the war, Foreign Minister in Berlin. He asked me to a meal and took me to his consulate, which occupied the whole floor of a modern office building and whose official staff, adequate in itself, was strengthened by bright young volunteers from Hamburg and Bremen.

Later on in my stay a German farmer and his family were wiped out by bandits and I asked Hintze what he was going to do about it. "Why nothing," he said. "I am here to make good relations with Mexico, not trouble." I recalled that remark six years later when the detection of Germany's offer to give Mexico part of the United States if Mexico would help Germany to win the war had a good deal to do with bringing American neutrality to an end. But at the time I dismissed it as a typical bit of Teutonic cynicism.

Luckily when the war broke out the Germans found themselves the victims of the impetus of their preparations, whereas we, having done nothing, had freedom to maneuver. One of the first things President Wilson did was to issue his famous appeal to his countrymen to be neutral in thought as well as in deed. This was a reasonable move (though resented by us) to mitigate the danger of racial clashes in the big cities, as well as an intimation to the belligerents that systematized propaganda inside the United States would be unwelcome. We were able to heed the warning. The Germans were not. Their propaganda machine was already in motion. Doctor Dernburg, a former minister of the Imperial government, was on his way from Berlin, ostensibly to collect money for the German Red Cross but also to take charge of its office in New York, the staff of which was recruited from German shipping and other companies put out of business by our control of the seas.

The German ambassador, too, took a hand and misplayed it, with an ineptitude surprising in a seasoned and intelligent diplomat. He celebrated his return with the weird statement that Great Britain would have remained neutral had Germany been able to accept the conditions she demanded for so doing. He lectured Americans upon the danger to their interests in the Pacific implied by the Anglo-Japanese alliance, he engaged in grotesque apologetics as to the origin of the war, he enlisted prominent but ingenuous sentimentalists in transparent efforts to place the blame for its continuance upon the

Allies. "Nothing," I wrote home, "can apparently cure Bernstorff of his predeliction for teaching the Americans to interpret the war in a sense favourable to the allies." As for the American press, it was not long before it warned him that unless he behaved, he might be sent home. He was reminded that in 1793 Genêt, the agent of the French Revolution, had been deprived of his post on account of his indiscretions, though he was allowed to stay in the United States, where he married an heiress instead of going home to the guillotine. Chastened by warnings such as that, Bernstorff, after a few months, drew in his horns, and, as will be related, became as successful a diplomat as he had been unsuccessful as a propagandist.

Years afterward when we resumed our prewar friendship at Geneva, where the Bernstorffs had settled to avoid Hitler, he told me that my attacks in *The Times* had helped him in Berlin. To this I retorted, truthfully, that American disapproval of his publicity organization in their country had helped us in Washington to persuade London not to make the same mistake as he and his people had made.

Spring-Rice arrived back at the embassy with instructions to advise urgently as to whether we should set up a propaganda office in New York. He called a meeting with Jusserand, the French Ambassador, and Havenith, the Belgian Minister.* I was in attendance. The discussion was short and the decision definite. The Allies could not afford to follow the German lead. "Give Dernburg enough rope," said Spring-Rice, "and he will hang himself." And characteristically: "Those who cannot see the rightness of our cause aren't worth arguing

---

* I do not know why Bakhmetieff, the Russian Ambassador, was not there. Perhaps he was away. He would have been useless anyhow. He was a parchment-faced, monocled diplomat of the old school, fond of good food and wines and of administering conversational shocks. "Scratch a Russian," I heard a woman say to him at dinner. "Not necessary in my case, Madame, I am a Tartar." He was married to the sister of the millionaire owner of the then anti-British Washington *Post*.

with." The decision was accepted by London after some hesitation and no British propaganda office was opened in America until after she was in the war, and then with the consent of the State Department.

That did not, of course, mean that no effort was made to influence American opinion. Far from it. The Canadian novelist Gilbert Parker was, if I remember rightly, appointed to turn a propaganda hose onto it from London. Lectures and pamphlets were distributed; eminent Britishers like Bryce bombarded American friends with letters, wrote articles for the American press, and gave interviews to the American correspondents who swarmed across the Atlantic. The British in America and, indeed, many Americans did what they could to help. Prompted by Dawson I offered my services to the embassy; they were accepted and my unofficial press officer functions became semi-official. My messages to *The Times* ceased to be altogether objective. I tried to render the Wilsonian neutrality as palatable as possible. I made suggestions to Dawson about editorial policy. I wrote articles for American reviews and magazines. An old envelope contains some of them torn from the *Atlantic Monthly*, the *World's Work*, the *New Republic*, and so on. One of my pieces in the *World's Work* was entitled "The British Case" and was published along with Dernburg's "German Case." Others among those long-buried pieces are "Why the World Is against Germany" (after the sinking of the *Lusitania*), "England's Cabinet of all the Talents," "Tommy Atkins in the Field" (how I secured material for that article I do not recall), and various articles defending our contraband policy. When Raemaekers' famous anti-German cartoons came out in America I wrote the letterpress for them.

Looking into rumors, some fantastic, some plausible, a few true, was another occupation, for in those days of improvisation and trial-and-error it was eighteen months before an efficient intelligence organization was established across the Atlantic. Stories came thick and fast during the first months of the war. Interned German ships were on the point of slipping out of New York Harbor, German-American filibusters were massing on the frontier to invade Canada, the Germans had bought the *New York Times,* German-American bankers were sending gold to Canada hoping to cause the Empire to be blamed for upsetting the American economy, Bernstorff was plotting with so-and-so, something was going to be blown up somewhere, Dernburg was being financed by Hearst, and so on. Many of those tales interested me professionally; all of them intrigued the embassy, none of whose staff upon which the war had caused to descend a spate of unaccustomed tasks and problems had, with one exception, time to deal with them.

The exception was the naval attaché, Captain (afterward Rear Admiral Sir) Guy Gaunt. He was an Australian, a thick-skinned, bouncing fellow. His father had been chief commissioner of the Ballarat gold fields at the height of their turbulent prosperity. He loved adventure and the limelight and, entering the navy from the mercantile marine, had enjoyed both in the Pacific. He applied for active service when we went to war but was told to stay where he was. He then asked the admiralty for permission to branch out into what he called propaganda-cum-intelligence activities to be conducted from the office that as naval attaché he was opening in New York, where he was soon a familiar feature. People liked the breezy, self-assertive Australian ("impossible for me, dear boy, not to have a Rolls; must show the flag").

I had, however, an excellent ally in New York to assess his stories. I had never solved satisfactorily the problem of our part-time correspondent there. So early in 1914 Northcliffe settled it by giving the post to W. F. Bullock, the *Daily Mail* correspondent in that city. Printing House Square accepted the arrangement sourly as being yet another *Daily Mail* infiltration. But Bullock went to London and saw Dawson, who found him far better than he had expected. To me he was a godsend, the best of colleagues, and a first-class journalist who understood what to give *The Times*. He knew New York inside out and had fruitful contacts in every direction, among financiers, politicians, newspapermen, the police, and officialdom.

I felt, indeed, after a month or so that I had got my wartime duties into good trim. My telegrams to *The Times* were well displayed. Then suddenly Northcliffe cabled that the *Daily Telegraph* and the *Morning Post* were better served from America than *The Times*. I asked Dawson what was wrong. He replied that:

> You seem to me to be sending just what we want. American opinion is frightfully important . . . It is vitally important that you should remain at your post and keep us informed both publicly and privately . . . You know the situation here well enough to realize that you will always be at the mercy of some conflicting instructions. However, you have served us so splendidly that there is really no room for cavil in any quarter now. Personally I do not agree that at any time you were in danger of being beaten by the correspondents of other papers. I think you must take that as a curious form of stimulant.

A letter from Northcliffe followed: "You grumble at being marooned in Washington: but as a matter of fact you are doing a very great service to the Empire."

Thus I was anchored for the term of the war, which we realized after a few months was likely to last a good deal longer than anybody, save Lord Kitchener, had at first thought possible. An indefinite period of continual Washington lay ahead for F. and me. The Spring-Rices settled the problem of Paul

and the hot weather by promising room for him and his nurse
in the house they would be taking in New England for their
children. We could snatch days of respite with friends nearby.
And anyhow, visits to New York would have to be frequent.

When in Washington I got up very early, rode, or walked and
ran, before breakfast. I was at the office well before nine, and
thanks to the five hours' difference between American and
British time and the increasing slowness of wartime transmis-
sion was quit of it so far as cabling was concerned by lunch-
time. In the afternoons I would see people and occasionally
walk or ride again, or take F. and Paul into the country, or
drive out with the Spring-Rices and walk home with the am-
bassadress. In the evenings there was sometimes relaxation
in congenial company, or the interest of giving small parties
often for strangers or new arrivals from abroad, parties that
ran easily thanks to the excellence of the colored servants of
those days with their good nature, their impulsive interest in
one's affairs, and their cooperative resourcefulness. Another
great support was Mary Early, the elderly Irishwoman who
was Paul's nurse all our Washington years, growing blinder and
blinder, but lovingly careful of her charge, never complaining,
always helpful. The only time I saw her annoyed was when F.
and I stayed up several nights to nurse our dog Dan. Ought
not Paul to have all our love? She could not realize that Dan,
on a different plane, was a member of the family, another defense against the pressures and preoccupations that beset us.

Dan was given us by Ruth McCormick and was named after
her brother. He was a Scottish terrier puppy when he arrived
and grew into the most delectable of dogs, too long in the leg
to compete for prizes and too good a friend, anyhow, to be submitted to the indignities of cage and ring.

CHAPTER 8

Trials of the Wilsonian Neutrality

A MERICAN NEUTRALITY in the First War lasted slightly longer
than in the Second and must have been far more trying for
the representatives of the Allies in Washington. There were
no helpful American moves like lend-lease or the destroyers.
Instead there was continual controversy, criticism, and tension, which would have been intolerable had it not been that
nearly everybody around wanted the Allies to win, or at least
the Germans to be beaten.

The best, indeed, that could be said for the Anglo-American
relationship during those years is that there was never the
slightest fear of its degenerating into war as had happened
when England was fighting Napoleon. I shall never forget going into the ambassador's study one evening soon after his return
to his post after the outbreak of war. He had been depressed
and worried by much that was happening. There was the President's appeal to his countrymen to be neutral in thought as well
as deed; there was the agitation of a vocal and politically powerful minority of pacifists, Anglophobes, and pro-Germans for an
embargo upon the export of war supplies to belligerents, which
meant to the Allies as the British navy would blockade the Cen-

tral Powers. Where did the President stand? Did he, like Bryan, think that the danger of German dominance of Europe was of no concern to the Western hemisphere? The ambassador that evening was temporarily reassured. The President had received him with unexpected warmth and had said, with tears in his eyes (so I reported to Dawson), that a German victory would destroy everything that he was working for and that made his arduous life worth living. It would mean conscription for America and the end of free democracy.

Happy, though not for long, about Washington, Spring-Rice was soon worried about London. Cotton, copper, oil, and some other commodities produced in the United States had been of no great use to armies in the old days but were now of essential importance in total warfare, and the admiralty under Winston Churchill wanted to treat them as absolute contraband at once. But Spring-Rice saw that precipitate action might drive the cotton, oil, and copper people, all powerful in politics, into an unholy alliance with the Bryan pacifists, the Anglophobe Irish, and the pro-Germans, with the worst possible results (short of war) to the Anglo-American relationship. Caution, on the other hand, might pay generous dividends. The United States was beginning to be lifted out of an economic depression by the trickle of war exports already going to the Allies. Left to itself the trickle would become a stream, the United States would wax fat on war profits, an embargo by Congress on war material would cease to be "practical politics," and we should be able to blockade Germany with nothing worse to fear than speeches, congressional resolutions, and notes of protest. Spring-Rice got his way. Cotton was not made contraband until the summer of 1915, and a few weeks later the success of the first British war loan in the United States showed that Wall Street had no intention of allowing war trade to suffer from lack of funds. The first phase of the contraband controversy was over. Looking back at it all, I wonder whether Spring-Rice's success does not entitle him to be considered as, perhaps, the last ambassador to shape vital policy at home by the cogency of his argument and by his personal influence.

In the second phase the ambassador was less successful. London, to put it roughly, steadily strengthened the blockade with both eyes upon the practical present. We in Washington urged that friction would be reduced if it spared at least half an eye for the legal past and followed as closely as possible the precedents set by the North in the American Civil War and even by the United States in the Anglo-American war of 1812. Experts in the State Department inclined, privately, to this view. Contraband became more than ever one of the principal subjects for my dispatches, private letters home, and above all for my memoranda for Flanagan, the leader writer. Their erudition impresses me when I read them again. But they were only the work of a reporter with excellent sources of information. In Washington, besides Spring-Rice, I had Robert Lansing and his principal assistant Frank Polk at the State Department. Both were lawyers, both anxious to avoid friction, and both my personal friends. Polk took Lansing's place as counselor of the State Department after Lansing succeeded Bryan as secretary of state in the summer of 1915. Lansing was a specialist in international law. Polk was fresh from the practice of law in New York, and the speed with which he imposed himself upon the State Department and the diplomatic corps made me wonder whether diplomacy was such an esoteric profession as it is sometimes claimed to be.

I was fortunate, too, in the friends I had outside official circles to whom I could turn for advice. Of these the principal were ex-President Taft and Elihu Root. Both were great lawyers and both had strong views coinciding with ours in Washington. I passed these views privately to Dawson and he asked me to try to work them up into a symposium that could be published. Taft and Root were reluctant to publish anything that might embarrass the British government, however foolishly they thought it to be acting. Root, however, wrote me a letter that he told me I could send on to my editor in confidence. He said that:

> The view which is expressed in the memorandum you sent me is substantially identical with the views which I have been expressing in private for a long time. It has seemed to me that much trouble would be avoided if Great Britain were content to plant herself on the broad grounds taken by this country in the Civil War, which covers the whole field of trade prevention, both as to incoming and outgoing goods, and included neutral ports within the field through the doctrine of the continuous voyage. Once planted upon that ground, the right to accomplish the object sought would be beyond controversy and all the rest would be a mere matter of lawyers' dispute about details, just as we disputed about details during the Civil War and had litigation about them such as the Springbock case and the Peterhof case.

Dawson showed Root's letter to those responsible for the blockade without effect. Order in council followed order in council. Cruisers hovered off American ports; American ships bound for neutral European countries were intercepted, detained, and searched in British ports; mailbags were rifled, letters opened. American firms suspected of trading with the enemy were blacklisted; American exporters had to have the ultimate destination of their goods vouched for by British consuls. American surgical rubber was seized on its way to Germany; German canaries on their way to the United States, etc., etc. Injured traders protested to Washington; Washington to us. Our replies, though sometimes dilatory, were always polite. The administration, nagged by its exporters and by our enemies inside and outside Congress, was less polite. I wrote to Dawson about "vicious but, luckily, unpublished" communications.

We on our side had greater grievances. One was the President's patience with Germany's murderous submarine attacks upon shipping that might be carrying cargoes to the Allies; the other was his advocacy of the compromise peace the Germans wanted, especially toward the end of the period of American neutrality. The Germans started their submarine campaign in retaliation for our blockade early in 1915. In May the *Lusitania,* the biggest liner afloat, was torpedoed with heavy loss of lives, including those of Americans.

I remember the shock of the news as though it had come yesterday. F. and I were at coffee after lunch when somebody rang up from the office of the Associated Press saying that they had just heard that the *Lusitania* had been sunk. "There goes Britannia's trident," F. exclaimed. On the day of her departure from New York the newspapers had published a warning from the German Embassy that Americans would do well not to enter the war zone in ships of the Allies. The warning was discounted as a piece of Teutonic intimidation. The Germans had already torpedoed some merchant ships without notice. But nobody, not even Bernstorff, he told me in afteryears, thought that giant liners would be so treated.

Then came another bulletin; many passengers including Americans had lost their lives. Would that mean a rupture of relations and perhaps war between the United States and Germany? I had already made up my mind that it would not. After an American tanker had been torpedoed with loss of life a week or so before, I had written home:

> The President is determined to avoid trouble. Public opinion is scared by the possibility of war. You must expect nothing from the United States. It is by no means certain that even the destruction of an American liner and the loss of a few hundred American

citizens would produce war, though it would produce a terrific clamour.

It was easy to write this privately but less easy to convey to the public with a minimum of damage to American feelings and to British temper that not even the sinking of the biggest passenger ship on the Atlantic and the death of Americans would elicit from the President more than a note of protest.

Luckily for me a few days later the President made his famous "too proud to fight" speech and the first of his series of *Lusitania* notes was dispatched. The crisis was over. Professional satisfaction at having been right conflicted in my mind with regret that Germany had got away with it. Would she get away with it again?

She did. The *Arabic,* another liner, was submarined, again with loss of American life, a few months later.

My first telegram allowed readers of *The Times* to think that the President would not be compelled to break off diplomatic relations with Berlin and did not dismiss the possibility of war. Nearly the whole of the responsible American press took the same line. I, especially, had a good excuse. The American secretary of state felt the same way and told me so on the night of the news. F. and I were dining with the Lansings. The other guests were General and Mrs. Crozier; the general was the head of the Ordnance Branch of the War Department.

After the women had left the dining room, Lansing cross-questioned Crozier about American military preparedness and derived scant comfort. There was also discussion as to whether the United States would be able to meet her own requirements without interfering with the flow of war matériel to the Allies. Later on, as we said good night, I wished the secretary of state all power to his diplomacy, and he replied gloomily that he thought the time for diplomacy was over.

President Wilson thought differently. Berlin made gestures

conciliatory enough for the President to send another note and for me to telegraph to *The Times* that the President "is extolled almost ubiquitously for having secured peace with honour at the hands of a bellicose nation by nothing but the patient use of words."

After that there were plenty of submarine atrocities, as the headlines called them. But, with one exception, their impact was easy to report. Washington protested, Berlin prevaricated, Bernstorff backed up his masters with effective effrontery, stalwart Americans led by Theodore Roosevelt abused the President's pusillanimity, and nothing happened until the sinking of the *Sussex,* a cross-channel steamer, again with loss of American lives. The President showed his teeth: there was a real "crisis"; Berlin drew back, and from the spring of 1916 to the autumn its submarines were in the diplomatic background.

One naturally sympathized with the American desire to keep clear of the European conflagration. Nor did it seem fair at first to cast stones, considering our own insular inability to recognize the German menace till too late. But by 1916, though I made what case I could for it in my writings, the Wilsonian neutrality had become very hard to bear. The President, as Spring-Rice used to complain, was like a man hanging onto the coattails of a friend fighting to protect everything both believed in. Had he forgotten what he had said at the beginning of the war? — that a German victory would be a deathblow to American democracy. And, besides hanging onto our coattails, he was pressing for a negotiated peace, which would be tantamount to a German victory as it would leave the militarists in power. Such were the feelings of the nationals of the Allies among whom I moved.

It was the same in London, where I spent a few weeks of the summer of 1916. A scattering of people among whom were Dawson, Northcliffe, Sir Edward Grey, and some of his subordinates in the Foreign Office made allowances; a handful of pacifists, radicals, and advanced thinkers approved of the President's desire for a drawn war, but, generally, ignorance, bitterness, contempt, and ridicule prevailed. The muddled, murderous battles of the Somme were then at their height. An Englishman and an American were looking at a newspaper. "Some fight," said the American. "Some don't," said the Englishman, and turned away. It was disconcerting to discover how little trouble even members of the government took to understand the constraints and inhibitions, personal and imposed by his obedience to public opinion, which made the President's policy what it was.

I attended a small lunch while in London at which Lloyd George, soon to be Prime Minister, and A. J. Balfour, soon to be foreign minister, were the principal guests. Lloyd George's attitude toward the President was neither informed nor respectful. What, he asked with a sneer, had Woodrow Wilson meant when, after the sinking of the *Lusitania,* he said that the United States was "too proud to fight"? I replied that he meant that the United States was too massive a country to be hustled into war. "Why then did he not say so?" I explained that it was because he sometimes failed to think out beforehand the key phrases of his speeches. Lloyd George expressed surprise, asserting that he always framed his key sentences in advance. Balfour blandly asked whether that applied to what he had said about Balfour's friends and relations at Limehouse (he was referring to a speech made by Lloyd George some years before in which the privileged classes had been roughly handled). "Certainly," said Lloyd George, "certainly." After that America passed out of the conversation but speechmaking continued to be discussed, and the two great men agreed regretfully that Winston Churchill would never be the orator he ought to be as he prepared his speeches too meticulously.

All the columns in *The Times* in which I had tried to de-pict and explain the balanced neutrality of Washington seemed to have been quite useless and I again asked Northcliffe whether he could not find somebody else for Washington and release me. He was not sympathetic and a few days later sent me a characteristic letter:

I am just off for the war or should have liked to have had more talk with you.

Regarding as I do the possibility of the war and its issues dom-inating the rest of our lives I cannot too strongly impress upon you the feeling we all have in Printing House Square that your place in the war is in Washington and I hope you will not dally with the thought of remaining here and going into the army. Of my organization some 3,000 have gone and 40 members of *The Times* editorial staff are already at the war; and I am sure that, had I the allocation of their services, I could have made better use of them than has been effected by the War Department . . .

CHAPTER 9

Woodrow Wilson Promises Peace

BACK IN THE UNITED STATES I went inland to describe the presidential campaign, then in full swing. It was another depressing experience. The ardent sympathy for the Allies so prevalent among one's friends in the East became less and less noticeable the further west one went. Neutralism ruled the roost. "The first thing you must realize about this city is that we are neutral." This was said to me in Cleveland by a leading citizen, and it was typical.

The campaign was dull and uninspiring. Woodrow Wilson went with the neutralist tide. Charles Evans Hughes, who had resigned from the Supreme Court to become the Republican candidate, did not dare to strike out against it. Wilson promised peace and prosperity if he were reelected and warned that a Republican victory would mean war. Hughes shirked the peace or war issue as far as possible. Only Theodore Roosevelt, back in the fold of Republican orthodoxy, and a few others urged preparedness against a threatening worst:

> In default of definite issues [I wrote to Dawson] the President's peace and prosperity stand will help him immensely. His pacifism, his record of fine phrases and vague aspirations are all most

representative . . . Provincialism prevails. Cleveland is worried because Detroit is getting ahead in population. Brooklyn is bothered because Boston beats it at baseball . . . Even Theodore Roosevelt is as one declaiming to an almost entirely empty theatre. All the applause he gets comes from a class of thinkers who might perhaps fill one row of the stalls.

All this I diluted into an article for *The Times*. I did not like doing so and was much relieved when the copy of *The Times* containing the article was followed by a letter from Dawson saying that he had had "tribute to its excellence from American friends" and that a leading American journalist had found it "unflattering but astonishingly true." The American journalist was Roy Howard.

Woodrow Wilson was reelected and the next two months were grimmer than ever. Berlin evidently thought that the time had come for a supreme effort to secure through American mediation the speedy peace it needed. The German chancellor publicly called for negotiation and said that Germany would join the League of Nations. The speech was well received in the United States, save by the stalwarts led as always by Theodore Roosevelt. Even the *New York Times*, though it soon recanted, advocated a "drawn war" in an important article.

That was at the end of November. Some weeks of confusion followed. The Germans supported argument by intimidation. Even before the President had been reelected they displayed the ability of their latest submarines to blockade American ports. One of them suddenly appeared in the harbor of Newport in Rhode Island, a naval station and fashionable summer resort, and, after staying as long as it legally could, put to sea and sank British and neutral ships within sight of the shore. The sensation was intense; the President lay low. The sinkings had been within the rules of war.

Worse was to follow. Just before Christmas the President
asked the belligerents to define their peace terms. He explained
that, according to the statements they had so far made, they
all seemed to be fighting for much the same ends. Theodore
Roosevelt called this "immoral." But on the whole the country
approved. The Allies answered by stating their war aims and
asserting their determination to achieve them. The studied
moderation of their language bore no relationship to the anger
behind it. Even that was not the worst.

After a month of note writing and of speeches and statements
on both sides of the Atlantic, the President went unexpectedly
to Congress and made his famous "peace without victory" address, which Theodore Roosevelt promptly proclaimed was
like saying, after Lexington and Bunker Hill, that there could
be no real peace if the forces of George Washington were
victorious. The British estimate of the American mentality
sank below zero. Even the imperturbable Dawson wrote to
me: "I fancy that 'peace without victory' is destined to live as
a phrase side by side with 'too proud to fight'. The broad difficulty with all this woolly idealism is that the American people
show no symptom whatsoever of being prepared to suffer anything for their ideals. That is what makes them so intensely
unpopular in England."

Just about then I had my one and only meeting with Bernstorff during the war. It was in the lift of the Metropolitan
Club. I entered the lift from an intermediate floor on my way
up to the dining room where the Allies were shepherded to
tables near the door of the big room and the Central Powers
to the far end of it. Bernstorff was alone in the lift. He winked
and smiled at me with complacent superiority. I bowed with
self-conscious solemnity. The ambassador had reason to be
pleased with himself. He had become the dominating figure
of the diplomatic corps. His silly statements and interviews
two years earlier had been forgotten in favor of the patient in-

genuity with which he had helped the President tide over the *Lusitania* and other submarining crises, and he was now enthusiastically applauding the idea of "peace without victory."

The Germans, however, against his earnest advice to do nothing to antagonize the President, soon put "peace without victory" out of the question by brutally intensifying their submarine campaign. The new campaign was announced early in February 1917 and two months later the United States was in the war.

Years afterward Bernstorff said to me that if Germany had been reasonably careful, the United States would have remained neutral indefinitely, in which case the chances for a negotiated and "reasonable" settlement would have been good and there would have been no Treaty of Versailles and no Hitler. But those "idiots in Berlin gambled upon starving the Allies into subjection before the United States was ready to help them — and lost."

I spent more days in New York than I did in Washington that critical winter of 1916–1917. The Atlantic cables were clogged and communication was so slow that in Washington I was forced to get my telegrams almost off before the New York papers arrived, which was an impossible situation, as the more unpalatable the news became, the more I used quotations from the American press to convey it. In New York I lived at the Belmont Hotel, where I had a small room and bath that cost *The Times* $2.50 a night. I got up at about 5:30, went across to Grand Central Station for coffee and doughnuts in a workmen's café in the basement, and returned to my room with a sheaf of newspapers and got my telegrams off by ten. Normally this banishment to New York would have been inconvenient, but as things were, it had a great advantage, namely that, as I told Dawson, "I have the American Government in tabloid form in a modest flat five minutes from my hotel."

The "American Government" was Colonel E. M. House,

the President's most intimate friend, his assistant, adviser, and roving ambassador. House worked persistently for a close Anglo-American understanding and felt that it was worthwhile giving the correspondent of the *London Times* what help he could, with the result that a friendship sprang up between us that more than made up for my lack of contact with the President. I can see him now as he sat at his tidy desk those winter mornings lifting the telephone that connected him with the White House and the government departments to secure him the latest information on this or that — a neat, gray, mousy, mustached little man with a high stiff collar, gentle, imperturbable, and omniscient.

House had had much to do with Woodrow Wilson's election to the presidency and could have enjoyed any office from that of secretary of state downward he might have fancied. But he preferred to work unobtrusively in the shadow of the great events that he helped to shape. He was a Texan, and his fortune, though modest, was sufficient for him to indulge his bent for *éminence grise* politics, first in his own state and then in the national field. The President's bitterest enemies respected him. I do not recall, if indeed I ever knew, what part he played in the Mexican business, but the President's mistakes leading up to the rejection by the Senate of the Treaty of Versailles were made either without consulting him or against his advice.

Willie Wiseman's presence there was another advantage that New York held for me during that winter. I have described his precocious incursion into Anglo-American affairs together with its political background at length elsewhere.* But something of what I said must be repeated here, for from 1916 onward he was a most valuable ally of mine. Sir William Wiseman was a young baronet just turned thirty when he arrived

* *The Road to Safety,* Derek Verscoyle, London, 1952.

in the United States at the end of 1915 to organize a British intelligence and counterespionage service. He had had business connections with the United States and Mexico before the war. He had entered the army and had been gassed in Flanders. We were soon in close contact and I used to try to tell him what was happening or brewing in Washington. But within a year the tables were turned and he had become, next to House, my chief source of information about high American policy. He was more deeply in the confidence of the President and his adviser than any other foreigner and most Americans and remained so until after the Peace Conference.

Woodrow Wilson and House, irritated though they were by the British blockade, were convinced that the world would have to be rebuilt after the war on an English-speaking foundation, and meanwhile believed that the best hope for American mediation in the war lay in close touch with London. And as 1916 wore on they felt that there was no close touch. They thought their own ambassador too pro-British and Spring-Rice too emotional for impartial and dispassionate communication. About their own ambassador they were wrong. The United States was never better represented in London than by Walter Hines Page. The trouble was that he saw from the first what the war meant and how it had to be ended.

Against Spring-Rice they had a case, for he did not always practice in Washington the patience that he had so successfully preached to London. He never completely recovered from the illness that had marred his debut as ambassador. He was grossly overworked in an understaffed embassy. He felt the war intensely. He saw it as a struggle in which neutrality was immoral. With nerves on edge, he sometimes let this opinion appear in inappropriate circumstances. Toward the end of 1915 he told Lansing and House that American opposition to our blockade meant the sacrifice of civilization and democracy upon the altar of ephemeral national interests. "Is the better sense of the United States to prevail or does the United States mean to join Bulgaria in ranging herself on what looks for the moment like the winning side? Were she to do so, she would earn the imperishable contempt of the British world." The quotation is from the letter in which I repeated to Dawson the account of the conversation that the ambassador, worried as to whether he had gone too far, had given me. He told me that House had made a scene, but that Lansing had simply replied that the United States was bound to look after her material interests. After those interviews his relations with the administration deteriorated steadily, and House in his unorthodox way began to cast around for some British official in close contact with the embassy with whom he and the President could talk freely and comfortably. The first man he sent to the White House to be vetted was Guy Gaunt, the Naval Attaché. Gaunt was promptly rejected. He told the President, then in the middle of his "he kept us out of the war" campaign, that it was high time for the United States to come into the war. In relating the conversation Gaunt said that it was left to him to do most of the talking.

Wiseman was House's next choice. Spring-Rice gave him a letter to deliver to House by hand. Wiseman was kept in unexpected conversation for a couple of hours. Other meetings followed and Wiseman was passed up to the President. Their first encounter took place at a reception in the Pan American Building in Washington to which Wiseman, F., and I had gone together. Wiseman was presented to Wilson and after a long conversation was asked to lunch by the President next day. After that he had the freedom of the White House, a privilege enjoyed by no other foreigner. I asked long afterward how he had managed it. He said that it was because he professed liberalism and never got emotional as the British and French ambassadors did.

Wiseman soon moved into the apartment building in which House had his flat, saw the colonel all the time, and more than once when House went abroad accompanied him as a sort of secretary acting as a go-between with British ministers and officials. They went well together, the elderly Texan and the youthful product of Winchester and Cambridge. They were both quiet and unostentatious, the type of men who pass unnoticed in the street, but impose themselves upon a room. No strain or urgency disturbed their impassivity.

Spring-Rice wisely felt that, as the Americans had offered him a plank to bridge the chasm that had opened between him and them, he had better accept it. Wiseman was given a room in the chancery to use when in Washington and the ambassador said to him sardonically, "Do what you like, go where you like and don't feel it necessary to tell me anything you think I ought not to know." After America entered the war, Wiseman was invaluable as a liaison between the President and House and the British on both sides of the Atlantic.*

* A full and accurate account of Wiseman's Anglo-American activities is given by W. B. Fowler in his *British American Relations, 1917–18 — The Role of Sir William Wiseman*, Princeton University Press, 1939.

CHAPTER 10

Woodrow Wilson Forced to Fight

I was in New York when Berlin challenged the President's
pacifism by announcing the resumption of indiscriminate
submarining at the start of 1917 and Bernstorff was given his
passports.

I hurried to Colonel House to put the obvious question. He
thought that hostilities were inevitable, but not at once. The
President would give Germany every chance of reversing a decision that could only lead to her ultimate defeat. He had upon
his desk a copy of *The Times* with a dispatch of mine doubt-
ing the President's ability to bring the United States into the
League of Nations, a project which was coming to the front and
which appealed strongly to me. He hoped that I would do my
best to prove myself wrong. The stability of the eventual peace
would depend largely upon the willingness of the American people to forget old traditions and prejudices and join the British
in insuring it.

House was very right about the President's slowness. The
peace at any price people were strong, headed by Bryan. But
slowly they weakened. I oscillated between New York and
Washington during those anxious weeks and I remember Bryan

remarking to me and others that if it had to be war, he hoped it would not be before the Allies had taken the fight out of the Germans. American pride and trade began to suffer. American ships cowered in port. Roosevelt and the realists gained strength. We intercepted the famous Zimmermann telegram and gave it to the President, who was growing more and more uncomfortable. He consented to American merchant ships arming themselves. But as Franklin Lane said, he moved like a glacier.

The address to Congress with which he inaugurated his second term of office was still indecisive. Ten days later the Russian Revolution broke out, the tsar was deposed, Kerensky became head of the government. Lansing said publicly that the last obstacle to "viewing the war as one for democracy against absolution" had been removed. Four American ships were sunk on consecutive days. Theodore Roosevelt demanded the rescue of the United States from the "intolerable and humiliating position of sheltering behind the British Fleet." The President remained inscrutable and it was rumored that he had disapproved of Lansing's remark. Then suddenly on March 21 he summoned the new Congress to meet on April 2. It was taken for granted that he would ask it to declare a state of war with Germany. But what sort of war? Many, as I told Dawson, feared that it would be "all state and very little war."

I had recourse to House to discover how far the President had been impelled down the road to active hostilities. House gave me permission to pass on what he told me to readers of *The Times*. "The President," I started by saying, "does not believe that the United States should embark, at any rate until there is an overwhelming popular demand for them, upon extensive military preparations. He would for the present concentrate upon the protection of commerce and upon co-operation with the Allies in an economic and commercial sense; he would do everything possible to help the flow of supplies across the Atlantic; one of the reasons why he shrank from extensive military preparations was the fear that they might deprive the Allies of desperately needed material that the American forces would not be ready to use until the war was over."

Much the same was being published in the American press. It infuriated the stalwarts. But I felt that at home it would not go down too badly. At the moment what we most desperately needed was more shipping to offset growing submarine sinkings and money at a less ruinous rate of interest than Wall Street was charging us. Also I was glad to place squarely upon the President's shoulders the sole final responsibility for American policy. That was on March 21. There followed ten days of noisy controversy, the stalwarts crying "forward," the pacifists and pro-Germans "back." An excited, apprehensive country groped in the dark with hardly a glimmer of governmental leadership.

On April 2 the capitol was surrounded by swirling crowds. Thousands of antiwar agitators, many with guttural voices, mingled with the sightseers. Troops and police were everywhere. The stalwarts were less in evidence than the pacifists and pro-Germans, but more confident. A Western senator said: "I may be getting ten pacifist telegrams to one patriotic one, but the latter come from people I know and who count in the community." Rumors flew about that the President was on the point of appearing. Nothing happened, and as the afternoon wore on it began to be thought that he would not come that day. So I went home for some food. As we sat down to dinner the telephone rang to say that the President was about to leave the White House. I hurried back to the capitol with one of the secretaries of our embassy who had been going to eat with us. A soft, damp spring night had fallen. As we turned into Pennsylvania Avenue the capitol came into view, floodlit upon its hill, serene and imposing, a more reassuring symbol of America than the milling crowds, the troops, and the police. The President with his escort of cavalry clattered by us as we were arriving and I was hardly in my seat in the press gallery before he entered the chamber.

Senators, members of the House of Representatives, judges of the Supreme Court, many decorated with small American flags, rustled to their feet for a moment. Then in a profound silence the President began to speak with measured eloquence and deep emotion. The silence did not last long. Approving roars reverberated when he said that the United States would not choose the path of submission; they grew when he pledged unqualified support to the Allies and their cause. "Mr. President, you have expressed in the loftiest manner possible the sentiments of the American people," said Senator Lodge, the bitterest and most contemptuous enemy, personal and political, that Woodrow Wilson had at the capitol.

It was, indeed, too emotional an occasion to be convincing. That was very much the view of the press gallery. Everybody in it was preparing his patriotic piece; leader writers all over the country would soon be tapping out editorials to match. But could the President effectively and promptly lead the country into a war out of which he had been telling it a few months before that it ought to stay, and for participation in which he had done less than nothing to prepare it spiritually and little to prepare it materially? It was soon evident that these doubts were justified. Congress declared a state of war; bills were introduced for selective conscription and for a vast loan more than half of which was to be relent to the Allies. There was talk of a few troops showing the flag in France. Then confidence began to be sapped by confusion and the conscription bill ran into danger. Bryan's pacificist-isolationist gang openly opposed it and the pro-Germans and Anglophobes exerted hidden influence.

Then out of the fog of censorship there appeared British, French, and Italian missions. A. J. Balfour, who was now foreign secretary, headed the British Mission, and Viviani, a prominent politician, the French, with General Joffre as his military colleague. British circles were nervous when the personnel of our mission was imparted to us. The French, we thought, would be all right; the square opposite the White House was named after Lafayette, and Joffre was the one general on the side of the Allies who had caught the American eye.

But what of Balfour? London's treatment of Ireland was more unpopular than ever with all classes of Americans. The execution of the leaders of the Easter Rebellion in Dublin had been followed by the hanging of Casement, who was thought to be more deserving of the madhouse or perhaps prison than the scaffold. And now at the head of our mission was the man who, as chief secretary for Ireland a generation before, had been called "Bloody Balfour" on account of the firmness of his measures against the nationalist extremists. We need not have worried.

Balfour's personal success was absolute. Wherever he went he conquered. He was invited to address Congress — the first British subject to be so honored. One was afraid that his audience might dismiss him, with his tall stooping figure and his lackadaisical manner, as nothing more than a picturesque specimen of an effete aristocracy. Far from it. Swaying backward and forward, hands on the lapels of his frock coat, hesitating in speech, he soon had the chamber under his spell. It was a triumph of the exotic and unexpected. Woodrow Wilson in one of the galleries leaned forward in evident appreciation of a fellow-artist. Irish sympathizers had planned a demonstration. It did not come off. Medill McCormick, after the meeting, gave me a sheet of paper on which was printed, "Ask Mr. Balfour: Why are you called 'Bloody Balfour'?" Medill was one of the supporters in Congress of home rule in an undivided Ireland. The leaflet had been scattered fruitlessly about the chamber. "So that is the worst your tough friends can do," I said to him. "Your man has disarmed us," he replied. "He is some salesman."

The behavior of the French and especially Viviani's obvious jealousy of Balfour came as an unpleasant surprise. The little Anglo-French community in Washington had lived through the trying years so comfortably together. The two ambassadors and their wives were close friends. Their subordinates formed an equally congenial group. There was only one French correspondent in the town, Georges Lechartier of the *Petit Parisien,* and when his paper sent him around the world, it was natural that I should take over his work. But with the arrival of the war missions competition for money and material and therefore popularity began to corrupt cooperation.

In one thing, however, we and the French were in agreement and that was our dismay at the unreadiness of Washington. Nearly everywhere good intentions and good men were in danger of being defeated by chaos. The Americans on their side had not realized how perilous the position of the Allies was, owing to the wholesale destruction of their shipping, details of which had been kept secret, the collapse of Russia, the massing of German troops in the West, and so on. During the waiting period between Bernstorff's dismissal and the declaration of war I had on the whole exaggerated in *The Times* the importance of the embryo war plans then under discussion. I did this to meet House's desire that *The Times* should try to curb British impatience with American slowness. Now, however, that America was in the war it seemed to me that frankness would be in place, that in the end it would certainly do harm to raise false expectations. So I told a great part of the truth in my dispatches and waited anxiously for the London reaction. Dawson soon reassured me:

> One or two of the radical papers, e.g. the *Star* of last night, enclosed, have been complaining that you are not sufficiently enthusiastic about the American effort. Of course I know, as any one with any friends in America knows, that you have been absolutely accurate and also very discreet. Nothing has done so much harm in this war as vainly pretending things are better than they really are . . . obviously you are going to get some of the odium which we have all had in our turn for telling the naked truth; but I am sure you do not care a rap about that.

Then suddenly I was snatched away from journalism. It did not take Balfour long to see that a strong personality was needed as permanent head of the British war mission. The war Cabinet agreed, and Lloyd George decided to send out Northcliffe, not only on his merits, we suspected, but also to put the Atlantic between himself and a formidable critic at a difficult period of the war. And Northcliffe grabbed me to be his "bottle-washer." He made me secretary of the war mission. Officially this did not mean much. The war mission was already organized to a certain extent in the sense that it consisted of a number of departmental commissions each with its own American opposite number. My real job, I soon found, was to act as Northcliffe's personal factotum in Washington. It was neither an easy nor a pleasant job save that I knew most of the Americans with whom it brought me into contact. It involved going behind the backs of our own people, though I always told them when I was doing so. But worse than all, it upset my useful and wholly delightful relationship with the ambassador.

Spring-Rice hated the arrival of Northcliffe. Northcliffe seemed to him to represent everything in twentieth-century England that set his teeth on edge. The *Daily Mail* was blatant and common (a newspaper written by office boys for office boys,

Lord Balfour, another representative of the fastidious old order, was said to have called it), his political methods blatant, vulgar, and dangerous, and his personality impossible. All this and more was poured out to me on the ambassador's being informed of my chief's appointment. Before then he had more than once indulged in the same sort of abuse and I had tried in vain to rebut it. Thus on Northcliffe's arrival I found myself between two grindstones with a vengeance. Northcliffe on his side was contemptuously tolerant, which made things a little better, but Spring-Rice concentrated his wit upon denigration and a sort of passive obstruction, which strained, though did not destroy, our friendship and did not help the British standing in Washington.

It was a heartbreaking business: a head-on collision between the old diplomacy of the professional ambassador and of the roving missions of Cabinet ministers and special envoys that the airplane has since so much facilitated. And on this occasion the new method won, as I will show, and as I hope I can also show, largely on account of the selfless way in which Northcliffe suborindated himself to the common good. I met him at quarantine when he arrived, and what struck me most in the conversation we had as the ship went on to her dock was the seriousness with which he was taking his mission. He called it the most important task of his life — failure now to insure maximum or greatest measure of American help in shipping, finance, matériel, and men might well mean deadlock in the war and deadlock would be tantamount to defeat.

CHAPTER 11

Northcliffe and Reading in America

THE SUMMER OF 1917 with Northcliffe in America was a period of mixed satisfaction and worry for me. Northcliffe was exacting but immensely stimulating; he cleared the air in Washington like one of those cool days of wind and sun that from time to time alleviate its summer heat. Our personal relationship developed from a good proprietor-subordinate relationship to real friendship, and I was touched after his death to discover that he had left me a small legacy.

If Northcliffe made others sweat he never spared himself. He saw that only one thing really mattered — to help the United States put her full weight into the war. She must be made to see — and the President especially — that her material contribution to victory took precedence over an idealistic peace. He would never listen to my arguments for the League of Nations, i.e., I suggested that leadership in it might justify our waning Imperial power. Next to getting the United States into the war, our first task, he used to say, is to make those people in London realize that the United States is now top dog and will remain so after the war. I do not think he foresaw the disintegration of the Empire — he showed no interest in Indian nationalism — but he did say to me that in time Canada might well outstrip England as its center.

As a matter of fact, the unfriendliness of the embassy started a train of events that a year later made the Anglo-American partnership a soundly going concern. The first of these events was Northcliffe's refusal to settle in Washington. He said that he hoped by making New York his headquarters and only visiting Washington on special occasions, he would lessen friction with the ambassador. His decision dismayed the leading members of our war mission. Washington was becoming the center of the war. Everything depended upon American money, men, and matériel and they upon Washington. The loan situation that the Washington Treasury had taken over from the New York bankers was particularly delicate and complicated. Procurement, too, had shifted largely from private hands to Washington committees. André Tardieu, the French Commissioner and a friend of mine from Paris days, had settled in Washington as had the Italians and Russians. He attacked me one day about Northcliffe's retreat to New York. I had my answer. Northcliffe had just extracted Rufus Isaacs, then Lord Reading and Lord Chief Justice, from an unwilling government to take over finance in Washington (he had successfully negotiated a banker's loan for the Allies in 1915); Northcliffe was now going to pay much more attention to propaganda. Tardieu did not like this news. He was trying none too scrupulously to whip up American opinion to support the French claim for money and matériel, and he knew that Northcliffe and Reading would be a formidable pair of competitors. Reading's arrival not only to take over the loan difficulties but to report upon the embassy situation was the second step toward effective war collaboration between Washington and London.

Northcliffe's self-appointment as British propagandist-in-chief was personal, unofficial, and irregular. He felt that it was thus that he could best contribute to the winning of the war. It has been said by people who ought to know better that he accepted his American mission for self-aggrandizement. Nothing could be further from the truth. Of course the American limelight was centered upon him. But he was always asking others from the Prime Minister downward to come out and share it.

I recall very clearly Northcliffe's announcement of his propaganda plans. It was made to Wiseman, Geoffrey Butler, and myself. Butler was a young Cambridge don of great charm and intelligence who had come out as pressman for the Balfour mission and stayed on to start (with the consent and encouragement of the State Department) a small propaganda office in New York. Northcliffe told us, as he told many others in those days, that he understood the Americans and they him. The press was at his feet. Every word he uttered would be lapped up, editors everywhere were his friends or itching to become so, reporters would surround him wherever he went. And he meant to travel. He had no intention of being tied to New York and Washington. Rotary Clubs and other audiences would clamor for him; he would write articles, give interviews, hold private conversations. The public hardly knew what the war was all about. When it knew, it would galvanize the government into effective action.

Northcliffe's main theme was simple. I heard it weightedly expounded at the Washington Press Club soon after his arrival. He dilated upon the immensity of the British contribution of the war, upon the large proportion of American money lent to us that we had relent to our allies, the need for the United States to mobilize all her resources if the war was to be properly won, how our resources were being mobilized, what we required from America, the folly of putting steel into skyscrapers when it was needed for ships. He traveled vigorously

to Chicago, Detroit, and other big cities. He proffered advice
to everybody from big industry down to housewives. At Detroit he placated Henry Ford who earlier in the war had
headed a fatuous peace pilgrimage to Europe and was now
irritated by bureaucratic muddling in London over some machines he was selling us, and I was surprised when I was instructed to extract from a Foreign Office bag copies of "Cobbett's
Rural Rides" and the "Letters of Tennyson" and send them on
to Ford.

There were of course indiscretions. There was a public ad-
monition of the President; things were said in private that
reached the whispering galleries of the Capitol. The President
complained to Wiseman, the ambassador said, "I told you so,"
and I wrote sadly to Dawson about our master's "unbridled
and damaging publicity." I was wrong. The annoyance it
caused the government was trivial as compared to the good it
did in the country. Northcliffe to the public was not a high
official behaving improperly but a great British newspaper
magnate, telling what the war meant in striking and intelligible
language. If Balfour had the success of the exotic, Northcliffe
had the success of the familiar. Like the Hills, Harrimans,
Carnegies, and Rockefellers of those days he had climbed to
the top with nothing but brains, personality, and initiative to
help him.

Lord Reading arrived in Washington early in September
1917. I saw nothing of his skill as a negotiator during this first
visit, but it was soon evident that if anybody could sort out with
the Treasury Department the tangled skein of Anglo-American
finance, it would be Reading. After a few weeks I told Dawson
that:

> Reading is doing very well. He has had more effect on the
> Treasury than three months of the sort of mixed representation
> we have been having. His relations with Northcliffe are excellent.

Indeed it would be strange if they were not. Northcliffe is so obviously bent upon subordinating himself to the common good.

As a matter of fact the cordiality was one-sided. Northcliffe
accepted Reading unreservedly as a colleague and equal, reported to London in glowing terms about him, and spoke enthusiastically about him to all and sundry. But the Liberal
politician never really trusted the Conservative newspaper
proprietor. I did not discover this until years later.

In November 1917 my chief and Reading embarked upon
the same ship for London behind an ineffective screen of melodramatic secrecy. Anglo-American money troubles were over
for the term of the war. Northcliffe, who had been hankering
after England for some time, said that he would soon return.
But it was Reading who returned as ambassador and head of
the war mission. This was the right arrangement, though
sadly marred at the start by the brutal brusqueness with which
Spring-Rice was recalled and by his sudden death a few weeks
later. Reading could not have contributed to the awakening
of America as Northcliffe did, Northcliffe could not have assisted the American government to take advantage of the
awakening as Reading did, and no professional diplomat could
have performed either task. The journalist was needed for the
first; the lawyer-politician for the second.

Reading was back at the embassy at the beginning of
February 1918. It was a bad moment. Though the country
was arousing itself, Washington was still in a mess. Nine
months of belligerency and good intentions had not cured the
administrative confusions of war procurement. Nerves were on
edge, frustrations were converging upon the capital from all
sides, the President was known to be still hoping for a compromise peace, a vast accumulation of stuff for the Allies was
piling up at the docks (a state of affairs which I said constituted
"the greatest triumph the Germans have had on the seas").

The Shipping Board was muddling its building program, material was short, labor slack, the Congress restless, the railways in bad shape, the Republicans playing "spiteful politics."

Lord Reading remained about six months in the United States. Before he left Washington in August 1918 I sent Dawson a long letter part of which follows:

Reading ought to be sailing in about a fortnight if his plans are allowed to hold; and Wiseman and I agree that it is up to you and everybody else at home to give him a really good Press. He has done wonderful work out here. In six months he has restored to the Embassy all and more of the prestige that it ever had. He is today the one Ambassador who counts. If the Allies have something important to say to the U.S., it is he who sees the President. The other Ambassadors lurk on the door step and listen to what he has to tell them and scuttle like messenger boys to their chanceries to telegraph it home to their Governments.

It is he more than anybody else who has kept our financial relations with the U.S. straight. It is to him that the first credit for Hoover's great work in saving us from the threatened food crisis this spring belongs. When he arrived here he saw that nothing in his instructions was more urgent than the tackling of the food question. He made it his business to meet Hoover and McAdoo at a really momentous interview in which he successfully brought to bear upon them all his powers of persuasion and proved to them that the war might be lost if they did not do what then looked like the impossible.

Roughly, this meant greatly increasing American exports at a time when the railways seemed unable to manage any more traffic, when Hoover and McAdoo were not on very good terms and when muddling seemed ubiquitous. After the interview McAdoo allowed Hoover to put the transport of food to seaboard into the hands of a remarkable Western railway manager, Conrad E. Spens. Spens, however, could not have cut the knot had not Reading again been on the spot. He found that the Allies' grain contracts were at sixes and sevens. Nobody seemed to know how things stood.

Reading organized the necessary machinery. He got down from

Canada and New York the best grain people he could find. He called into being a Committee to co-ordinate the needs of the Allies. We were thus often able to load more than 50,000 tons of grain a day. The very greatest credit is due to Hoover who stands head and shoulders above the other American war executives. But I do not believe that without Reading we should have been able to tide over to the spring.

Man-power was the next great crisis that he had to face. Though the problem was in some senses a French problem he took the lead at the White House and elsewhere with the result that we have since seen. (The arrangements for the American forces in France.)

Reading has been able to do all this partly because he is such a great worker but still more on account of his personality. He is regarded almost with awe in the Departments as well as with liking and trust. His politics (the fact that he is a Liberal) and his position at home have both been a great help to him but still more useful have been his extraordinary power of lucid and cogent statement and his charm.

Reading was helped by the great German offensive toward Amiens in March 1918. I was away with him in Chicago when things were at their worst. On our return a note awaited him from Wiseman fresh from the White House to say that the attack had been a great shock to the President. He had never believed in this much-advertised offensive. He had thought German morale was low. There had been a readjustment of opinions and of hopes to which he had "stubbornly clung in spite of much advice to the contrary." Wiseman, incidentally, continued through Reading's embassy to act as a confidential link with the President and House.

I must have introduced to Reading most of the journalists who frequented Washington. I have a letter from one of them thanking me for making him known to "the most impressive Ambassador I have ever met. I wonder if you realize how much it helps your country to be represented by a self-made man who is also a Jew and your Lord Chief Justice. It shows that you are a real democracy where brains and character can go to the top."

For me life had been less of a strain under Reading than under Northcliffe. I no longer had to spend about two nights a week in the train between Washington and New York, as the direction of our affairs was at last centralized in the capital. My journeys now only took place at arranged intervals, mainly to talk to Butler about publicity matters in regard to which we were our own masters, for Reading, beyond being accessible to journalists and making occasional speeches, bothered but little about propaganda.

Butler and I did, however, have a valuable ally at the embassy in the unusual shape of the principal assistant military attaché. This was Arthur Murray (afterward Lord Elibank). Northcliffe was indirectly responsible for him. Soon after my chief's arrival I reported to him that a friend in the War Department had complained to me that our military attaché, an excellent and popular officer but lacking experience of the present war, was no match for the experienced French officers whom Tardieu had brought with him and who were feeding the Americans with news and comment from the fronts with an obvious French slant. My friend asked whether it would be possible for us also to provide them with a flow of up-to-date information so that the progress reports on the war prepared for the President could be better balanced. I reported this to Northcliffe who exploded to London, and within a month a major general fresh from the front arrived at the embassy with Murray, who had also seen active service as his assistant. Murray, besides being a professional soldier, was a Member of Parliament with an insight into foreign affairs sharpened by a term as parliamentary private secretary to Sir Edward Grey before the war. Like Eustace Percy he went far afield in the exploration of the American scene, making friends with all sorts of people. His influence at home also helped.

In war mission matters my immediate chief was Sir Henry

Babington Smith, whom Reading had brought out as deputy high commissioner. He had been private secretary to a viceroy of India, whose daughter he married, a leading official in the British Post Office, and president of the National Bank of Turkey. He was a man of charm and great ability. Among British and Americans alike he won golden opinions. He lived across the street from us in what had been Northcliffe's flat, and F. and I saw much of him. Upon the table on which I write lies one of those Victorian elephant tusk paper knives, which his widow gave us after his premature death. Another member of Reading's staff who made his mark in a different manner was a captain from the Indian army called Kennedy Crawford Stuart. Stuart was a pleasant fellow. His popularity in society was, however, modified by a tendency toward ill-judged witticisms. "Why, Captain Stuart, are you so popular in Washington?" asked an important hostess. "Oh, I suppose because I am middle-class myself." A still unprintable riddle-jest about the President was afterward to impinge most inconveniently on Anglo-American relations at the highest level.

After about four months with Reading and Babington Smith I persuaded them to allow me to return to my proper work. I argued that I could be just as useful to the mission as *The Times'* correspondent as I was in its office. I continued to represent the Ministry of Information and had "The British Pictorial Service," as Butler's organization was called, painted on my office door under "The Times, London," and hired an extra typist. I felt like a blackbird released from a cage into a fruit garden.

For Butler my chief duty was to keep in touch with George Creel and his Committee of Public Information. Creel was a journalist from Denver and easy to work with even when he and Butler disagreed. The only real fuss I recall with him was over some alleged Bolshevist documents that he got hold of and published. They pictured Lenin and Trotsky as paid puppets of Berlin and were tremendously played up by the American press. London doubted their authenticity and refused to give them out. But my summary of them in *The Times,* to the extent of nearly a column, got past our censor, which took the edge off Creel's disappointment. I continued to help Butler with the priming of lecturers and other British travelers, not all of whom were to the good, for there was little control over passengers to the United States during the First War. This laxity of control did, however, produce one entertaining incident. A few British subjects liable to conscription sought refuge in American cities where as often as not they hinted at secret service duties. Prompted by these whisperings the Germans approached the soldier servant of one of Wiseman's assistants for a blueprint of their organization. He was told to accept its purchase price and was furnished with a blueprint. On it were the names and addresses of a number of these shirkers. Their rooms were ransacked and some of them ran off to Canada and were caught up in the army. When the Germans discovered that they had been fooled they caused a message to reach Wiseman that it was really too bad of the English to make fun of serious matters. That was while America was still neutral.

The two most effective unofficial propagandists we had were both Irish. One was Shane Leslie, a cousin of Winston Churchill. The other was Sir Horace Plunkett, whom I regarded as the best Irishman of the time. His efforts to settle the Irish question are a matter of history. His efforts on behalf of Anglo-American understanding are less well known. He was often in America during the war. He had been a rancher in the West when young and spent energy and money telling that part of the continent what the war was about. Spring-Rice paid particular attention to him, and he was one of the very few foreigners whom the President received. Like Spring-Rice he used to disapprove of my intercourse with so-called pro-Germans. I remember his coming to tea with us and being shocked by finding pro-German literature in the room. Leslie was invaluable to us all on account of his contacts with the leading Irish Americans and especially those in the Catholic hierarchy.

My first telegram to *The Times* was headed boldly "America in her War Stride." Enormous preparations were on foot for the 1919 campaign, which was expected to take the Allies, reinforced by vast American armies, into Berlin. The President was making his influence increasingly felt in the conduct of the war and the preparations for peace. He was arguing authoritatively with the Allies about intervention in Russia. The Allies wanted to launch an army against the Bolshevists in the Far East. The President disapproved. The army would have to be mainly Japanese, its requirements would weaken the all-important Western front, the Japanese were unpopular in America. Also one suspected that the President, having burned his fingers in Mexico, might well shrink from plunging into Russia unless the bulk of the population clearly desired intervention. And of this he and his experts were doubtful. His appraisal of the Bolshevist strength was more realistic than that of London, though his hope that Bolshevism might calm down into tolerable liberalism was sadly misplaced.

All this and more I tried to explain to *The Times* in another long telegram. It never appeared. I thought that my old enemy, the British censor, was at it again until I learned that the telegram had never reached London. I complained to Creel. He showed me his censorship instructions. They were eminently reasonable. I consulted Wiseman, who in due course sent me a copy of some ultrasecret instructions that had been given to censors by a higher authority to suppress all matters indicating serious dissensions among the American people, to scrutinize carefully all attempts at interpreting the President's opinions on probable actions, and, oddly enough, to suppress all reference to suffragette pickets at the White House. This did not bother me. There was no copy on the suffragettes, there were no serious dissensions among the American people, and if the President did not desire to be discussed, well, it was a pity. I should have liked to say something nice about him for a change. As it was I told Dawson privately how I thought he stood:

> He is popular with the country — or perhaps I should say trusted and respected rather than popular. He is felt to have all the strings in his own hands and to be manipulating them well. To him is given credit of having made the United States count in world affairs. Even the hyphenates (the Irish and German Americans) like him in spite of the way in which he has trounced them. They are inspired by the hope that Destiny has sent him to lead the United States to the forefront of the nations and to relegate us to a back-seat.

Woodrow Wilson was indeed the pivot of the world in the late summer and early autumn of 1918. The Central Powers looked to him to alleviate the consequences of inevitable defeat. The Allies relied upon American strength to hasten victory and consolidate peace. We in Washington felt that he was bound to dominate the peace negotiations if he continued to play his cards with the judgment and decision he had recently been showing. I wondered whether I and others had not after all been wrong in regarding him as an ignorant and self-willed doctrinaire in foreign affairs. His balance and grasp of realities seemed to have been developed by the pressure of great events. Then suddenly they failed him, and his slow and tragic slide into the abyss of discomfiture and defeat commenced. The famous armistice negotiations, initiated without consultation with the Allies and against the opinion of his countrymen who by then were in the mood to march to Berlin and enforce unconditional surrender, were his last success.

CHAPTER 12

The Old Order Strong in Paris

B EFORE THE ARMISTICE negotiations were over Woodrow
Wilson appealed to everybody to vote Democratic in the
November congressional election on the ground that a Republican victory would hamper him in the peace negotiations. The
country was shocked by what it considered a poor return to
the Republicans for the support they had shown him as the
national war leader, and the Democrats saw defeat before them
in an election already doubtful.

I was embarrassed. Here was a case where I might well run
foul of the secret American censorship. I played safe (unneces-
sarily as Creel told me a day or two later) and telegraphed
The Times that "the Democrats might be defeated," explaining
that this would not diminish the American will to win the war
as the Republicans were just as determined upon total victory
as the President. But I told Dawson that the appeal had produced intense bitterness and that the President might wish that
he also had come to coalition when confronted by peace problems.

To Wiseman, who was in attendance upon House at the Supreme War Council at Versailles, I wrote after the Democrats
had been defeated:

The Republicans, if they don't play the fool, should win the next [presidential] election. But you will find that they will give the President such legislation as he needs for the peace-settlement, including the ratification of treaties, unless, of course, they are antagonised by being allowed no representatives at the conference.

The Republicans were soon antagonized in just that manner. To the amazement of everybody Woodrow Wilson appointed a delegation to the Peace Conference that contained none of their leaders nor a single representative of the Senate. No more suicidal act of political folly could have been imagined. The Republicans would soon control the Senate; treaties, under the Constitution, had to be ratified by a two-thirds vote of the Senate. There was also general regret that Woodrow Wilson should have so gratuitously deprived himself of the assistance at Paris of men like Lodge in the Senate or Taft and Root outside it. And what chance was there, people asked, that a man who could make such flagrant misjudgments in the field of home politics could cope with the tried and wily statesmanship of the Old World. I recall Senator Lodge's split-mindedness: on the one side his satisfaction that his bête noire should have made such a fool of himself, on the other his determination not to allow the Republicans to embarrass the President while at the conference.

What caused Woodrow Wilson to flounder so fantastically? Soon after the armistice the French Embassy celebrated the occupation of Strasbourg with a party at which he made an unreported speech. The circumstances of the party are vague in my memory. I think some of us dined at the embassy and that afterward there was a small reception that the President honored. But the picture of him as he spoke remains vividly with me. I can see him standing behind a table, upright, pale-faced, self-satisfied. He started with some platitudes. Gazing at a British admiral in full uniform, he said that the war had done one great thing. It had made the Allies know each other better, and he quoted some author (Emerson?) to the effect that it was much more difficult to dislike those one had met than those one only knew by repute. Then he said in effect, "I am old enough to remember the rape of Alsace-Lorraine and my heart bled for the sundered provinces. How wonderful it would have been could I have known that I was to live to go to France as her victorious friend to play the leading part in their restoration."

Undoubtedly self-esteem influenced the President to take part in the conference as well as his crusading idealism. House, Lansing, and others advised him not to do so. House saw no objection to his visiting the allied countries and attending the inauguration of the conference but would have had him return to the White House and from that Olympus give a lead to public opinion when the occasion arose and thus maintain a supremacy that he was liable to lose in face-to-face haggling. As for the membership of the American delegation House did his futile best, before he preceded the President to France, to persuade him not to ignore the Senate and the Republicans. Had Woodrow Wilson listened to him at that juncture and had he sought his advice later, the United States would, in my judgment, have accepted the Treaty of Versailles and the other peace treaties and would have been, but only for a short time, a member of the League of Nations long enough to influence European reconstruction for the good.

I followed the President across the Atlantic in the old *Mauretania,* the sister ship of the sunken *Lusitania,* in company with Dick Oulahan, the Washington correspondent of the New York *Sun,* and Mark Sullivan, the editor of *Collier's.* Dawson had cabled a few weeks before that he wanted me as one of his team at the conference. He invited F. to come along as the guest of *The Times.* She refused this generous invitation. She did not want to leave Paul, and her exertions in local war activities had induced illness from which she never quite recovered.

I reached London late one evening. I deposited my things at Printing House Square where I was sleeping and had a short but shattering conversation with Dawson. He said he was near the end of his tether with Northcliffe, who was suffering from something approaching megalomania as well as bad health. He asked me to keep this to myself. A few days later Northcliffe appeared suddenly from the country where he had been nursing a bad throat. He looked tired and harassed, not at all the man he had been in America. I wondered whether his immense expenditure of energy there might not have started the decline. In America he had been reasonable and open-minded about everything save living in Washington and his determination to be the British propagandist-in-chief. Now he was didactic, domineering, and prejudiced. "Northcliffe," I wrote to F., "though most affectionate to me and full of questions about you and Paul, is having a bad fit of Napoleonism."

I had sent *The Times* a dispatch during the armistice negotiations attempting to explain what the President was after and saying that the popular demand then running high for unconditional surrender did not imply that he wanted a hard peace, that he was, indeed, grateful that the Allies seemed to be swinging around to the view that vengeful diplomacy was out of place. Northcliffe asked me why Washington thought that the Allies were inclining toward a soft peace. I said it was partly due to a speech by Lord Milner that had by no means reflected the "hang the Kaiser" hysteria Northcliffe was whipping up. This produced a tirade against Milner. Nobody took him seriously; he belonged to the scrap heap of the past. And Milner, as everybody knew, was the man upon whom Dawson leaned above everybody for advice.

London itself deepened my depression. It seemed to be taking victory so sadly. The streets were greasy and badly lighted, houses needed paint, the parks were untidy, the people looked drab and tired, and food and fuel were short. The German guns lining the Mall and the German airplanes on the Horse Guards Parade were about the only signs of triumph. It was a relief to be in the country for Christmas where there were family affairs to deal with, my mother having died in the course of the preceding summer.

Paris seemed less warworn than London. The impending conference created an atmosphere of expectancy. A general tidying-up was in progress. I installed myself in the Hôtel Castiglione where *The Times* had taken what I described to F. as a "magnificent suite." I had not been in Paris since I said goodby to Lavino in 1906, and the Castiglione presented quite a contrast to the third-rate, restaurantless hotel I had put up at in those days. Next morning I found *The Times* office in the Chaussée d'Antin just as I had left it, except that one now walked in without ringing the bell. In it were the rest of Dawson's conference team, namely, Wickham Steed, the foreign editor, and George Adam, the Paris correspondent.

I did not stay long at the office that first day and, after accepting an invitation to dine with Steed, went to the Hôtel Crillon, the headquarters of the American delegation, to pay my respects to House. He fixed an appointment for a long talk next day and secured for me a pass that gave me entry to the hotel, the use of its restaurant, and, what was more important, the freedom of its cigar stand. House sang Steed's praises as well as those of Northcliffe. At dinner that night I found that Steed was equally under House's spell and felt that Dawson's fear that he would neglect the English-speaking side of the conference was exaggerated. It was not, however, without some justification. "I am having some struggles of the friendliest sort with that impulsive crusader Steed. So far I have had my way as Adam backs me," I wrote to F. a few weeks later.

Steed was foremost among the ardent group of British godparents of the new states into which the Austro-Hungarian Empire was being carved up. Their leaders, Masaryk, Benes, and others, were his intimate friends. He fought their battles in conference circles with indefatigable tenacity and, as Dawson had apprehended, wanted more space for them in *The Times* than they deserved. Luckily, there was a safety valve at hand. Steed had been Northcliffe's principal lieutenant at Crewe House where my chief had conducted his propaganda campaign in enemy countries after his return from America. Northcliffe, like House, thought that Steed knew more about Europe than any other Englishman. Northcliffe told me that he, besides writing for *The Times,* would be doing lead articles for the Paris *Daily Mail.* Thus, Northcliffe gloated, those who read English in conference circles would have the benefit of Steed's sagacity over their morning coffee. Another safety valve for Steed's astonishing energy was the almost daily reports he sent Northcliffe on conference matters.

Steed was extremely good to me. He showed me his reports to Northcliffe. He lectured me on the politics of Central Europe and introduced me to the principal figures concerned with them. He amused me. He was such a deliberately dramatic figure. He was more continental in appearance than any of his continental friends. His French was perfect. So too I believe were his German and Italian. With his slim, neat figure, fine small features, and close-trimmed, grizzled beard, he only needed a monocle to be the perfect stage ambassador. He had served as *The Times* correspondent in Rome, Vienna, and, for a short time, Berlin. Like Lavino, his predecessor in Vienna, he had preached the inevitability of German aggression. He was as much in his element in Paris that winter as he was destined to be out of it in Printing House Square as Dawson's successor.

I did not, as Dawson feared, have to act as a shock absorber between Steed and the British delegation; there were no rows while I was there. But the cordiality was perfunctory. The

Prime Minister and his entourage distrusted Steed as North-cliffe's spy and emissary; the Foreign Office, which had been irked by his impetuosity as foreign editor of *The Times,* dis-liked his backstairs forays into their affairs.

Personally I could take no urgent interest in the drawing of the new map of Europe. Other things seemed more pressing. "The pity of it," I wrote somewhat pompously to F. after a few days in Paris, "is that in Europe racial and national aspirations threaten to obscure the fact that the world is asking for a real settlement on League of Nations lines and that a good part of the continent is waiting to be fed and put upon its feet." More than ever did I feel that in leadership in the League lay our best chances of regaining the supremacy that the war had cost us.

Partly for that reason I look back at the conference with mixed feelings. It was good to be at the center of affairs after the anxious years on the periphery of the war. On the other hand the League of Nations was my principal interest, professionally and personally. The drafting of its convenant was going well but under bad omens for its future. It was an experiment in internationalism, and the war had exacerbated nationalism. Old distrusts and ambitions had been stirred up and new ones created.

The obvious first task of the conference was the rescue of the starving parts of Europe, especially Germany. Here sheer urgency coupled with the fear of Bolshevism prevailed. "Bol-shevism," House said to me, "is coming westward. A barrier of contented self-respect must be interposed at all cost." The second task was the rearrangement of the map of Europe, and indeed of the world. The League could wait. That was, I soon felt, the prevailing view of the old diplomacy still strong in the foreign offices of the Old World in which the Wilsonian "New Order" was by many regarded as a transatlantic aberration that had to be taken seriously only on account of the strength of the United States. The League might be a useful center for people to meet and know each other and settle small problems, but for big ones, old-fashioned negotiations, meetings of ambassadors, special conferences, etc. There was much talk of that sort in Paris. Its strength and that of the old nationalism was soon to be proved. The French wanted special treaties with Britain and the United States to reinforce their Eastern frontier against a resurgent and vengeful Germany. The American and British representatives at the conference gave them the treaties; Washington and London repudiated them. Washington's action was natural and inevitable; London's uninspired and inexcusable, a first step in the somber series of commissions and omissions that laid the Continent open to Hitler.

In regard to Anglo-American relations my work was easy. It had looked in Washington and London as if there might be friction. The Wilsonian doctrine of the freedom of the seas seemed an ominous threat to harmony. Akin to it was American restiveness at the British claim to continued naval supremacy. The treatment of Russia, the blockade of Germany, the drafting of the Covenant, procedure at the conference, all carried germs of contention. Rivalry, too, was in the air. The reaction from the close partnership of the war had started before the war was over. The President's visit to England had not eased things. I remember Lord Robert Cecil's disappointment at not being given a serious opportunity for discussing the League of Nations.

House nevertheless was optimistic. He told me that "Great Britain and the United States would start the Conference seeing eye to eye with each other on all important subjects." There had, he said, been divergence over the disposal of the German colonies but compromise was already in sight. There had been arguments over the freedom of the seas and naval rivalry but "the trouble had been mainly started by Englishmen who proclaimed loudly that the British Navy had to be kept strong enough to lick creation." Anyhow, "economic necessity would soon scrap British pretensions to a two-power naval standard."

As for the Covenant of the League, the President presented its draft to the conference after about six weeks' committee work in which he played a leading and constructive part. It was once again possible, as during the preceding summer, to be eulogistic about him. It was not long, too, before he saw that if the League of Nations functioned properly and with all its members united against the aggressor, there would be no neutrals and in consequence no need to insist upon the freedom of the seas, which was the second of his Fourteen Points.

The controversy about British naval supremacy had boiled up acrimoniously at the preconference discussions. Lloyd George maintained that no British government could afford to abandon it and Wilson replied, through House, that the United States was prepared to build to the limit in competition. The naval confrontation was thus so serious and the need for Anglo-American harmony at the conference so urgent that the problem only came up inconclusively toward the end of the proceedings. Two years later, at the Washington conference for the limitation of naval armaments, Balfour accepted the inevitable, agreed to parity with America in important ships, and was made an earl for his pains.

Woodrow Wilson and Lloyd George had little in common save the ability to make great speeches and ignorance of foreign countries. (Lloyd George once sent for a member of the Foreign Office to ask about Egypt. The official said something about the fellaheens. "The fellawhats?" exclaimed the Prime Minister. "Are they a Trade Union?") The Welshman despised the American as a politician and was jealous of him as a national leader; the American distrusted the Welshman. During the Second War I used to wonder what would have happened to the Anglo-American partnership in the First War had the two men possessed the means of personal contact put at the disposal of their successors by air travel and the transatlantic telephone.

Smooth working among their subordinates neutralized these incompatibilities. Among the seniors in both delegations some were already friends and among the juniors friendships and a sense of common purpose soon developed to such an extent that the English-speaking members of some of the committees found it advisable to conceal from their colleagues the intimacy that existed between them.

The spectacle of the Empire in collective action also helped. The British delegation slept and ate at the Majestic Hotel. The hotel was not in itself an impressive place as compared with the American Crillon, and the food there was that of a second-rate English station hotel, the kitchen staff having been brought from home. But if the food was bad, the company that consumed it could often be impressive and I was glad to be frequently among it:

> I take a good many meals at the Majestic [I wrote to F.]. The other evening I was there with Frank Simonds as a fellow-guest. A.J.B. [Balfour] was giving dinner to that young Lawrence of the Middle East; Smuts and Botha at another table; a group of be-ribboned Indian officers at another; Borden of Canada, Hughes of Australia also present; several young Americans with British contemporaries. Even the hard-boiled Simonds was impressed.

Frank Simonds was a leading American journalist. He had seen the war coming and had studied the terrain where the main fighting took place and also the armies that were engaged, and I thought he overtopped the other American military commentators.

He was impressed to see Botha and Smuts, the two great Boer generals, happily consorting with their opponents of twenty years and less ago, as the trusted representatives of the youngest

of the dominions fresh from running the Germans out of Africa.
There, too, was the Indian delegation, their chief in a British
general's uniform, to answer the Indian nationalist propaganda
that Germany had been financing in the United States. Canada
at that time still figured in the minds of some Americans as a
colonial subordinate of England, yet there was Sir Robert Bor-
den, as impressive a figure as any at the conference, representing a transatlantic dominion that had lost more men in the war
than its great neighbor. And Hughes of Australia from the
Antipodes, less impressive than the others, rather deaf and
strident, but friendly, approachable, and not at all averse
from telling my American friends how much Australia had done
for the mother country at the Dardanelles and elsewhere,
though her population was less than that of some of their states.
The Americans liked him better, I think, than some of the
English did. Indeed, the only British figure to whom they, like
myself, failed to take was T. E. Lawrence, self-consciously conspicuous in Arab clothes. Various of my friends, notably Ronald
Storrs, admired him fervently then and afterward. But to me,
in my casual encounters with him, he was always an unsympa-
thetic enigma.

Dawson stayed with me for a few days soon after the opening
of the conference. We saw most of the people in the British and
American camps whom the editor of *The Times* ought to see,
with the exception of House, who was unwell. We discussed
the affairs of Europe with Steed and Adam, but in them Dawson's interest was perfunctory. He was John Bull incarnate
in the overheated cosmopolitan atmosphere of Paris. He was
contentedly ignorant of the French language, or pretended
to be, and amusedly scornful of the behind-the-scenes politics in
which Steed reveled. If he supported the League of Nations it
was because he hoped that it would bring the Empire and the
United States together as the custodians of peace. I told
Dawson that, interesting and educative as I was finding it all, I

did not think I was earning my pay and keep in Paris and asked
to be allowed to clear out for America as soon as the drafting of
the Covenant was completed. He said he would think it over,
and after his return to London wrote that:

> It was very pleasant to have those three or four days with you.
> Do not be under any delusion as to the value of the work you are
> doing. I thought your additions to the few notes I wrote on Sun-
> day were of the greatest possible interest and I am sure you can
> go on pushing some of the broader features of the Conference.
> Otherwise we might easily be let down over the British and Amer-
> ican points of view. You must of course go back with the Presi-
> dent but I want you to stay in Paris as long as possible.

Dawson's "few notes" were in reality a long and able dispatch
upon the conference machine, which he said consisted at that
juncture of "half a dozen great governments in miniature with
an interminable outer fringe of small delegates scattered sometimes at distances of miles from one another all anxious to
press their particular views without any obvious focus or
centre." The article was salutary. No international meeting
of anything like the same size had ever been held before,
and the confusion was aggravated by some of the delegations,
including the British, being, as Dawson pointed out, grossly
overstaffed.

The President left for America soon after he had presented
the Covenant to the conference. I followed him after spending
a couple of days in London and a quiet Saturday evening with
Dawson. He was his usual solid, imperturbable self though
he had in fact resigned but, as he explained in a letter that followed me to Washington, he could not tell me this, owing to a
pledge of secrecy. The blow was not the less heavy because expected, but was somewhat softened by my having found Steed so
agreeable to work with in Paris and by Northcliffe's having written to me from the Riviera that Steed had said the same of me.

CHAPTER 13

The Old Order Wins in Washington

O N THE NIGHT of my arrival in Washington we dined with the McCormicks. Medill, though only recently promoted from the House of Representatives to the Senate, was already one of its most active isolationists. Borah was there. Both were bitter about the President. They felt that he had betrayed his country in Paris and himself at home. They said that he was mismanaging his visit to Washington just about as thoroughly as possible. He had invited the Foreign Relations Committee of the Senate to dinner at the White House, but, according to Borah, a member of the committee, had been gruff and uninformative, and to his Republican guests unfriendly. As for the Covenant of the League, both senators were convinced that the Old World in general and British imperialism in particular had taken advantage of the "muddled mysticism" of Woodrow Wilson. Medill gave me a copy of a letter that he had just sent to some organization in his state of Illinois that disapproved of his hostility to the League. It ran in part:

> You are for the constitution of the League of Nations as presented to the Paris Conference. I am not. Since you are for the proposed constitution, you approve of giving the British Empire

six votes in the League to one vote for the United States. Upon what grounds do you justify giving the British Empire, in proportion to its self-governing population, twelve times the voting strength of the people of the United States? Is one Englishman twelve times as important as one American?

Medill went on that under the terms of the Covenant, there was nothing definite to prevent the United States being overrun by Oriental labor or European powers lodging themselves in Latin America. I used this letter in one of my dispatches. Everybody agreed that the Covenant would have to be altered for the Senate to accept it.

I stayed on in America after the President had returned to Paris for a couple of weeks to give *The Times* some idea of the aftereffects of his propaganda foray and of the amendments of the Covenant that would be necessary. In the last of a diffuse and repetitive series of telegrams I said that:

> To judge from the press and the utterances of public men one would think that the country was in a furore over the League. The polls that have been taken, especially in the Middle West, do not bear this out. Nowhere has the debate been keener than in Chicago; yet an elaborate poll taken by the *Chicago News* shows that, if opposition to the Covenant is less strong than the local Republicans make out, by far the most striking thing is the number of people who are not interested enough to have an opinion . . . The Republicans are trying to re-awaken for their own ends in this mass of indifference not only the old instinct for isolation but also the old distrust of Britain.

In April I spent another fortnight in Paris. I was not of much use to *The Times*. Steed had succeeded Dawson. Adam, with the assistance of one or two people on the foreign side of the paper, was carrying on smoothly while Steed oscillated between Printing House Square and the conference. I was, indeed, in Paris less for professional reasons than on account of personal affairs that I wished to discuss with Northcliffe, who had come north to Fontainebleau. So far as the conference was concerned my time was mainly spent in answering questions about the President and the Senate. The redrafting of the Covenant was nearly completed, and it was clear that the President would not secure the two alterations considered in Washington to be the most vital, namely, the abandonment by the British of six votes for the Empire as compared to one vote for the United States and the modification of the article of the Covenant by which signatories were pledged to protect member countries from aggression, if necessary by arms. Smuts and Hughes in particular were determined that the dominions should have their votes, and to most of those who believed in the League it seemed doubtful whether economic sanctions would be really effective without force in the background.

The President was losing ground owing to the failure of his Washington visit. Only against the Italian claim to the possession of Fiume was he making an effective stand. Rumors, damaging to him, as House was everywhere liked and respected, were rife that his relations with his adviser were deteriorating. Jibes at him in the French press provoked an official reprimand. Jokes at the transatlantic crusader had been current all along. Usually, and sometimes correctly, they were attributed to Clemenceau. At first they had been kindly, though cynical. There was, for instance, the well-known one of Clemenceau's surprise that Wilson should have fourteen commandments when the Good Lord was content with less. By April they had become acid. The favorite was Clemenceau's alleged reply to someone who could not detect much difference of meaning between "accident" and "tragedy." "But there is," said Clemenceau, "a great difference. If President Wilson fell into a well it would be an accident; if he was fished out of it, it would be a tragedy."

The New Order was being badly battered. I recall a lunch

with Sir Eyre Crowe, soon to be the permanent head of the Foreign Office, Esme Howard, and others. The gathering strength of the Old Order was discussed. Howard had just returned from some conference with officials of the new German Foreign Office. He said they were the same old Wilhelmstrasse gang. All they had done to mark the end of the Empire was to wear cloth caps instead of hats.

The matter I wanted to discuss with Northcliffe was my future; while in America he had told F. that if she wanted to be near Paul when he went to school and if I needed a change after the strenuosities of Washington, he would find something good at home for me.

We were of two minds about the change. Life in Washington was very congenial and would presumbly be easier with the return of normal conditions. Also Northcliffe was going downhill and Steed, as editor, was untried. There was a good deal to be said for still keeping the Atlantic between Printing House Square and myself. On the other hand F. was far from well, and in Washington it would be difficult for her to live the easier life that she needed. There was also Paul. He would soon have to go to a boarding school and afterward would come Eton and Balliol. Thus the scales inclined from the first slightly toward England.

I spent a couple of nights at Fontainebleau alone with Northcliffe. I was disturbed by his condition. He said that the Riviera had done him good, but there was scant sign of improvement. His throat (soon to be operated on) still bothered him, he was nervy and restless, his features had coarsened, he looked soft, fat seemed to be replacing muscle. There was a taint of decline about him. Lloyd George had just made his once-famous, overdone, but not altogether unjustified, attack on him in the House of Commons, and, when he told me that it did not worry him as his papers were always there while prime ministers came and went, this jarred upon me as a boast of ill omen. His views on peace-making were disturbing. He was obsessed by what he thought was the weakness of the conference and particularly Lloyd George toward Germany. He wanted Germany to be made to pay and pay.

About my own affairs, Northcliffe's first point was that I must stay in Washington until after the presidential election of 1920. Then, if we decided to come to London, I might perhaps take on the foreign editorship. Steed and I ought to go well together, he with his knowledge of Europe, I with my American experience. I already knew something about Canada, and the other dominions and the colonies could be visited in due course. He was, however, only thinking aloud and I was not to pass on what he had said to Steed. He wanted Steed to make his own decisions (their brief honeymoon was then at its most intense). He would, however, put the idea into his head. A few days later Steed told me that Northcliffe had spoken to him and said in effect that I could count on the foreign editorship.

I returned to Washington in June and took the family to the house at Marion whence the war had snatched me so abruptly five years previously. Marion, which I suppose is now overcrowded and vulgarized like other seaside places everywhere, was then the perfect spot for a quiet holiday. The small summer colony was compact and friendly. There were sailing and fishing in Buzzards Bay; one could row into the harbor after tea and hook small mackerel for supper or catch scallops in a landing net. One could bathe either in the bay or harbor. The former meant a rush from the house through a thicket or scrub and clouds of mosquitoes to an empty beach; the latter depended upon the hospitality of neighbors. I have many good Mediterranean memories of sea and sun, but none is surpassed by those of plunging into the clear, brisk water of Marion harbor and coming out on to a sun-warmed lawn to swallow oysters fished up from a little bed laid down by our host and wash them down with cocktails.

I did not enjoy these pleasures for long. I wanted to make a plunge into the Middle West to obtain some idea of what people in general were likely to think of the impending struggle between the President and the Senate. Before I left Marion I asked the fisherman from whom we hired our boat his opinion of the League of Nations. He inquired whether membership would compel America to take a hand in European affairs. I said that it might do so. He answered that in that case he was against joining, as Europe seemed to him like a bucket of crabs out of which it was as well to keep one's fingers. Across the Appalachians this clear-cut isolationism was then less prevalent than I had expected to find it. Though there was little enthusiasm for the League, most of the newspapers I visited and the individuals I talked to took it for granted that the United States would join it and thought lukewarmly that she ought to.

I was back in Washington about a month before the President. Congress was in session and the capital buzzed with discussion of more amendments. Few really wanted the League, but it was still the case that the President might recoup himself if he played his cards with prudence. It seemed at first that he might do so. He cast off the cloak of arrogant aloofness that he had worn in March. He visited the Senate and conferred with groups of its members. He saw the press and made a good impression. Compromise was in the air. In due course the treaty was sent to the Senate and referred to the Foreign Relations Committee, of which Lodge was chairman. It was soon clear that the President's new-found amiability had been adopted not to facilitate bargaining but in the hopes of inducing the Senate to accept the Covenant as it stood. The weeks passed, the deadlock tightened, the extreme isolationists gained ground again. The projected American and British treaties with France for the protection of her Eastern frontier gave them useful ammunition. So did the handing over to the Japanese by the conference of the concessions that the Germans had enjoyed in Shantung.

The President, too, postponed until too late the propaganda tour that in Paris he had planned to make soon after his return. It was September before he set out, and by then he had wasted his strength by argument in the summer heat, while the country had become thoroughly upset by all the domestic problems that war leaves behind it, now so familiar but then so unexpected and baffling. Prices continued to rise, housing was scarce, profiteering was prevalent, great strikes threatened, Negroes rioted. Making the world safe for democracy became less important to the ordinary individual than making the United States again a comfortable place to live in. Tired before he started, the President collapsed in the middle of his tour after a series of fine speeches before preoccupied audiences and was conveyed back to Washington a helpless invalid.

The next six months were surely the most bizarre that Washington has ever experienced. Executive leadership was never more needed and less available. Members of the Cabinet dealt with their affairs as best they could and met from time to time under the chairmanship of Lansing. None of them saw the President whose sickroom was guarded by Mrs. Wilson, the White House doctor, and a few others. A stroke or even insanity was suspected. The insanity theory was exploded by two senators who were allowed into the sickroom officially to discuss Mexico, which was as usual giving trouble, but in reality to investigate the invalid's state of mind. They reported that his mind was clear though he did not appear to be able to move at all.

It was noticed that Colonel House no longer visited the White House. Two explanations were bandied about. One was that Mrs. Wilson had always disliked House's influence over her husband and was now in control; the other was that the President had been jealous of his friend's popularity and influence in Paris. Anyhow the two men never met again.

Round about Christmas it was admitted that Woodrow Wilson had had a stroke and the admission was taken as a sign that he was improving. To Northcliffe I wrote:

> So far as one can gather, the President is about to come out of his shell to the extent of a more or less perfunctory share in affairs. I believe that the Treaty has been helped by the frank, if tardy, avowal that he has had a stroke, for these are a sentimental people.

I was wrong. The President came out of his shell but only to kill the treaty. The first thing he did was to send Lansing a letter reproaching him for unconstitutional action in calling the Cabinet together during his illness and to tell him that he would be "relieved of embarrassment" if the secretary of state resigned. Lansing resigned forthwith. The letters were published and the President's stock took another plunge. A few weeks later he wrote to the Democratic leader of the Senate so intransigently about further alterations of the Covenant that the last hope of saving the treaty vanished. I told Tyrrell that:

> The Treaty has been glissading steadily down over the snow towards the precipice and is now near its last leap. I see no chance for it. Now, as always, everything depends upon the President and, so far as anyone knows his ears are still back and the whites of his eyes still show. You can discount the stories of his recovery. He can only totter. Apparently the hallucination has been allowed to prevail that the League was really popular and that only the vile and ignorant obstinacy of the Senate stood between the United States and the leadership of the millennium. In the last days Baruch, McAdoo and Co. have been making desperate efforts to banish the illusion. Editors have been mobilized to write letters and so on.

In March 1920 the Senate voted, though not by a large majority, to return the treaty to the White House as unacceptable. The Wilsonian crusade in world affairs was over and America back in isolation. I was in the press gallery when the vote was taken. It was for me a sad occasion. I had hoped, as I have said, that America would come into the League and remain there long enough to help in the reconstruction of Europe. I also felt for the President, antipathetic as I had always found him. As a politician he had earned his defeat. As an idealist he had deserved better things. There was no taint of self-seeking about him. In foreign affairs ignorance had been his bane. Good intentions over the League had been frustrated by bad judgment, bad management, and bad health.

CHAPTER 14

The United States Finds Victory Sour

A STRANGE SIDE PRODUCT of Woodrow Wilson's collapse was the treatment accorded by the White House to Lord Grey of Fallodon during the autumn of 1919. There had been no British ambassador at Washington since Reading went home in the summer of 1918. This had not mattered much at first. The embassy was in the hands of a competent counselor and Wiseman was still there to act as a substitute for an ambassador in high matters. But now Wiseman was going back to private life, and with the impetus of wartime collaboration over, there was need for contact between Washington and London at the highest level. Hence, shortly before his ill-fated tour of the country, the President accepted with alacrity the suggestion that Grey should come over as a temporary superambassador.

House had got on so well with Grey while the latter was at the Foreign Office that he returned from one of his visits to London with a special cypher for confidential man-to-man communications. The President admired Grey as a great Liberal and a League of Nations man, and (so one was told at the time) blamed not him but the "city" for our hostility to his Mexican policy, while the stubbornness of our blockade policy he attributed to the admiralty. Grey, too, when he arrived soon after the President's collapse, was accompanied by Tyrrell who, on his previous visit to Washington when Spring-Rice was ill, had made an excellent impression at the White House and elsewhere.

Grey's mission came to nothing — officially. He was never allowed to present his credentials to the President and so remained no more than a private visitor. Week succeeded week without the slightest gesture from the White House. Sir Horace Plunkett passed through Washington and was asked to tea by Mrs. Wilson. This was natural. When in Washington Plunkett seldom missed a visit to the White House where interest in the Irish question was intense. But, if Plunkett, why not, as a matter of courtesy, should not Mrs. Wilson invite Grey to tea? And if the President could converse intelligently with the two senators, why should he not summon Lansing to his bedside to help him with the formality of receiving the ambassador? Was Grey's friendship with House the answer? This may have had something to do with it. But it was by no means all.

We soon discovered that the White House was justifiably annoyed by the reappearance with Grey of Captain Kennedy Crawford Stuart who, as already related, had launched — when out with Reading — an outrageous riddle about the President, and also a scandalous tale about one of his entourage. Both had reached the ears of the White House. At first unofficially and then officially (by Lansing) Tyrrell was told that there would be satisfaction in high quarters if Stuart were sent home, and one afternoon he summoned me to help him persuade Grey so to act. I cannot recall Tyrrell's arguments; I suppose they were the obvious ones. But I recall clearly Grey's reaction to them. Stuart would stay until he went home; Grey was not going to prejudice his career by dismissing him. But Stuart's stay would not be lengthy. He (Grey) had been thinking for some time that he was useless in Washington and had determined to depart before long. That was about a month before he actually left, taking Stuart with him.

Grey was wrong in thinking that his time in Washington was wasted. He was there for three critical months in the Anglo-American relationship. Reaction from the partnership in the war was in full swing. There was the accusation that we had bamboozled the President over the League and so on. There was jealousy over matters of trade. In the course of the war American pride had been titillated by grandiose plans for postwar expansion; it was now being discovered that such plans were easier to conceive than execute. England was suspected of stealing marches. It had been hoped that after the great ship-building activities during the war the American mercantile marine would again be in a position to compete with ours as it had done before the Civil War; it was now being discovered that this would be difficult on account of high wages and of the inexperience of management. At first it had been thought that the depreciation of sterling was a symptom of British weakness; it was now seen to be working for our advantage in the markets of the world. We were suspected (as I reported to Northcliffe) of designs to "hog" Russian trade by filling in the Baltic provinces with "stuff" ready to be poured into Russia at the first opportunity. A trade mission to South America under the leadership of an ambassador was taken as a sign that we were trying to get ahead of the Americans in their own hemisphere. Irish home rule was again to the fore. London had accepted the Wilsonian doctrine of self-determination; why was it not acted upon in regard to Ireland?

The strain would have been considerably greater but for Grey's interposition. The White House boycott strengthened his authority. People wanted to make up for it. He had countless opportunities of bringing into play his personality, prestige, and frankness. I must have introduced to him most of the journalists within reach who counted. He took infinite trouble over them. Not long before he went home, the Gridiron Club, that celebrated dining club of American journalists, gave him a great dinner. I wrote to Northcliffe (the fate of the treaty in the Senate was still in some doubt):

> I write sleepily this morning, having been up till past two at the first Gridiron dinner since the war. Grey was the guest of the evening and he made a most effective speech. The League, Ireland and everything else were touched upon with wonderful skill. His League argument was in the shape of a question as to what he would not have given to have had a commission of the Powers to refer to in 1914. It is the strongest argument one can produce here . . .
>
> Lord Grey is anxious to talk things over with you as soon as possible. He is anxious to get the following points well into people's minds. 1. The Senate should not be accused of repudiation. It is fighting the President largely on a constitutional issue. 2. We must make up our minds to something tantamount to the Lodge resolutions. We must admit the justice of the American claim that it would be unfair for us to use the votes of the Empire so as to give us a preponderating advantage.
>
> Lord Grey goes back because he feels he can be useful in getting this into the heads of the Cabinet . . .

Grey towered above the agitated turmoil of the leaderless capital, a massive figure of imperturbable sanity, whose rectitude and reliability usefully counteracted the somewhat different impression made by Lloyd George on American minds at the Peace Conference.

Another excellent British representative in Washington in the autumn of 1919 was the Prince of Wales on his first visit to America. I was also involved with him. The brains of his party were those of Edward Grigg, who had been attached to him after distinguishing himself as a soldier. Grigg came down from Canada in advance to survey the lay of the land. During the prince's stay I was called upon to brief him about the politicians and officials whom he was to meet and was impressed by the accuracy, charm, and tact with which the information I had imparted was brought into play. Politically a reception the National Press Club gave him was the most useful event of the visit. He made a short, simple speech followed by informal presentations. I stayed on into the night after he left and found the tough and cynical crowd really impressed not only by his speech but still more by the way in which he humanized the difficult business of shaking hands and saying the right few words. "That night," I told the readers of *The Times*, "the wires took the news to all parts of the country that a Prince could be democratic and a 'good fellow' and yet retain the dignity of his position."

Meanwhile the domestic situation worsened and gave me more to write about than the treaty, Lord Grey, and the prince put together. Discontent grew. It was found intolerable that a victorious crusade in a just cause should be rewarded by so much trouble. I recall only one incident that gave a little light relief to the social and industrial anxieties of that autumn. The Negroes in Washington, before the war so placid, were restless and there was rioting. A few days later the State Department protested to Mexico City about damage done to American interests in some disturbance. To this President Carranza replied that he was surprised that the American government should take so seriously his temporary inability to maintain order in a remote province when it was unable to keep the peace in its own capital.

Everything else was somber and threatening. I took full advantage of the limitless amount of space that *The Times* was ready to give to American affairs in the Northcliffian era. There were great strikes in the coal mines, the steel plants, and on the docks. Even the sedate railroad unions were restive. Small strikes broke out everywhere. My sympathy was with the men. Labor conditions were worse than those of England. Soon after America went to war a British labor mission came over headed by George Barnes, a member of the war Cabinet. They went on a tour to the obvious places and on their return I invited some American politicians to meet them at lunch. One of the politicians put the inevitable question — How did what they saw in America compare to what they had at home? "Do you want a straight answer?" asked Barnes. "Yes," said his interlocutor. "Well, if we had your conditions there would be revolution."

I was helped in my telegrams and articles by our friendship with Samuel Gompers and his quietly pleasant daughter. Gompers, though born in the East End of London, had for years been head of the American Federation of Labor. All through the war he was a resolute friend of the Allies, fighting enemy propagandists and saboteurs in the factories and urging total victory after America joined us. He was a small, frail man and these turbulent months bore heavily upon him. Nevertheless he found time to help me explain what the industrial ferment meant: full-blooded, passionate, sometimes unrestrained to the verge of savagery; so much more human and exciting than the struggle over the treaty, the snarling of the Senate, the silence of the White House.

The Times published everything I sent and displayed prominently a series of articles on what it called the "American Labour Ferment," articles in which I still feel a certain pride of authorship. But that was all. It was left to Pomeroy Burton of the *Daily Mail* to send me a note of congratulation on the "only sensible articles I have seen on the labour troubles." It was very different from what it had been when Dawson was editor and Northcliffe in good health.

Having assisted at the burial of the treaty I hurried with F. to

London to put Paul in school and find out about the foreign editorship. It was arranged that I should leave Washington after the presidential campaign, late in 1920, and take up that position. I accepted it with misgivings. Northcliffe, though as well-disposed as ever, was palpably going downhill. *The Times* was not what it had been during Dawson's first editorship. Dawson was in the center of affairs; he understood England, or at least those who governed her. Their doors were open to him as a friend and equal. He had his personal and political antipathies and predilections, but kept them in control. He recognized the limits of his knowledge. He never during his first editorship ventured rashly onto unknown territory as he did so disastrously in his second, over "appeasement" and Munich. He had a good opinion of himself but in an unobtrusive English way. He was English to the core.

Steed was English only in blood. In everything else he was foreign. Nothing, Dawson once wrote to me, will ever make Steed understand the English. He was as impulsive as Dawson was self-controlled and quite failed to grasp the value of moderation in British controversy. "What," said Lloyd George to me one day later on when I was in the Foreign Office, "what has happened to Steed?" I inquired what he meant. "Why," he said, "he hasn't attacked me for a fortnight and I don't like it. It looks as if he is learning British ways." In continental journalism, he explained, enemies were attacked all the time and on every pretext. Up to now that was how Steed had been treating him and it had done him no harm; rather the reverse. But if he starts the British game of attacking only at calculated intervals and even occasionally praising, then people will take notice. He must be stirred up.

The spring of 1920 Steed was indeed driving at Lloyd George and the government with unbalanced bitterness. *The Times,* somebody said, "no longer thunders; it shrieks." He was at

odds with the Foreign Office. "Steed, with that penchant of his
for categorical misjudgment," said Tyrrell. *The Times,* more-
ever, was not prospering under the new regime.

Why then did I not have second thoughts and stay on in
Washington? I did not do so mainly for reasons already touched
upon and partly because I was encouraged by people like Tyrrell and Philip Kerr (Lord Lothian), then the Prime Minister's secretary, to hope that in Printing House Square I might
perhaps mend some of those links with the outside world that
Dawson's departure had broken. Also Steed seemed genuinely
to want me, and lastly, if things went wrong, it would not much
matter. F. and I could do with a long rest.

Back in America I went to Chicago for the Republican Nominating Covention and on to San Francisco for the Democratic
Convention. They were dull preludes to a dull campaign. The
fire and fury of the last peacetime contests in 1912 were missing. Theodore Roosevelt was dead, Woodrow Wilson a hopeless invalid; the Republicans were bound to win. The conventions only interested me on account of friends in their arenas.
Medill McCormick was the progressive candidate for the
chairmanship of the Republican gathering. He was defeated.
Warren G. Harding, who ended so sadly, was nominated. Even
the stimulus of bitterness was absent. I traveled out to Chicago
with the McCormicks and we stayed with Medill's cousin, Harold McCormick. Conservatives and progressives mingled ami-
cably at his house.

At the Democratic Convention my friend in the limelight
was Franklin Roosevelt. He secured the vice-presidential nomination. He was still comparatively obscure outside New York
State and Washington. "A Roosevelt for Vice-President" was
the heading given by *The Times* to my telegram announcing
his nomination as running mate to Governor Cox of Ohio. He
flashed into prominence during the first session. A demonstra-

tion started in honor of President Wilson. State delegations picked up the poles that bore the placards with their names and began to parade. The New York State delegation in which the President had few friends "sat silent and sullen [I quote my telegram of that day]. Suddenly there was a disturbance round their placard and Mr. Franklin Roosevelt, the Assistant Secretary of the Navy, helped by a socialist ex-mayor of Schenectady, was seen wrestling with several fat politicians for the pole. Presently he won and part of the delegation perambulated."

I stayed that summer at Hyde Park while Roosevelt was resting after a long campaign tour. I wrote to Northcliffe that he was not at all sanguine about the election. "Harding," I said, "is pretty colourless, but Cox is a little cheap even for this year. The Associated Press man with him finds him like a beginner trying his hand in a small municipal election."

Northcliffe and Steed had told me to go to Canada from San Francisco. I had not been there since before the war and they thought it would be good for me to see something of the dominion and also to attend the Imperial Press Conference in Ottawa, before settling down in London.

My companion on this trip on which San Francisco was the first stop was our Military Attaché, Major General Keppel Bethell, a tireless man with a fine fighting career behind him. Our next stop was Vancouver. There the local newspaper proprietor took us in hand and we saw as much of that gloriously situated city and its surroundings in four or five days as the average tourist would see in a fortnight.

Bethell and I parted in the course of our journey across Canada but met again at Ottawa where we stayed at Government House and I attended the Imperial Press Conference. We then went on to New York to a palatial establishment on Long Island for the wedding of a daughter of the house to one of Bethell's assistants. It was an agreeable and luxurious occasion with an odd incident to top it off. Bethell and I were in the hall on the morning of our departure when a subordinate came up to him and asked his advice as to how to handle a butler who refused a tip on the ground that the butler's rank in the army had been higher than his own. Bethell sent for the butler. The butler said that he and his two footmen, London shop-keepers in civil life before the war, had held commissions in the same regiment and had decided, rather than serve behind counters again, to emigrate to the United States and prey on millionaires.

In Washington I evacuated (and hated doing so) the little house we had so happily occupied, sold most of the furniture, sent the rest to London, and lived at a hotel that then existed across the street from the Metropolitan Club. Before plunging into work I reviewed my tour to the West Coast and through Canada for Northcliffe. Here is a part of what I wrote:

> The contrast between the U.S. and Canada is like the difference between the crystalline St. Lawrence and that singularly muddy and unattractive river which owes its romance to Mark Twain. Canada has come out of the war braced and sanguine. America has come out of it softened and dissillusioned. She has missed the promised fruits of victory . . . Canada has her political problems . . . The point is that she is not worried or put off her balance by them. Her spirit is simply fine, though her critical attitude towards the U.S. is disquieting . . . It might have been thought that the million odd Americans who have taken up Canadian farmlands in the last decade would have had their influence against this tendency. All the information I got was to the contrary — that the American settler soon becomes an ardent upholder of Canadian institutions.
>
> The war has done a great deal to bring Canada together with the 'Old country' as well as to halt the movement for closer relations with the U.S. It has given the average man a fresh admiration for us. But it has not solved the Imperial problem. In a

sense it has aggravated it. There is very serious criticism that we do not pay enough attention to the Empire and are too much inclined to follow a too European policy. Dafoe, the great progressive journalist, whom you know, and a strong champion of an improved Imperial system, spoke bitterly to me of our subservience to the French who, he said, were bedevilling the world . . .

The difference between the United States I was about to quit and the United States I had entered fourteen years before was, indeed, striking. The sparkle and ebullience that had so excited me then had given place to disillusion, puzzlement, and depression. The cost of living was going up and up, war profiteers still flaunted their extravagance, Prohibition was beginning to poison the community morally and physically. The railways were still suffering from the strains of the war and the farmers were even fuller of grievances than usual. Wall Street, sensing depression in the air, sat strangely impotent among its moneybags. I unburdened myself about this to Northcliffe after again staying with the Roosevelts:

To spend a weekend as I have been doing with the Roosevelts who are the best American stock, as good as our best, and then come back to New York is an eye-opener. One feels that one has been with a vanishing race, a race which must be engulfed by what one sees in New York, by the teeming masses of poor, undersized foreigners in the sub-ways and down-town streets and by the representatives of the successful among those foreigners a generation later, by the profiteers who now swamp Fifth Avenue with their over-dressed grub-like women, people without an ideal or a thought, people whose sole interests are dollars, clothes and the latest leg-show.

In the industrial centres one sees the peril in another form and no less sinister one. One goes to the farmlands. One finds a better stock but I am always struck by its mental inferiority. But it is sentimental, easily moved and quick to forget. Climate or something seems to have done them a hurt. One has the placid Scandinavian becoming an hysterical socialist, and the Anglo-Saxons lending themselves to any sort of radical empiricism. Perhaps it is only a phase; but I think it is a dangerous phase, dangerous to the nation and others. The healthy influence of Theodore Roosevelt so noticeable a decade ago has died down after a period of ineffective leadership which is now to be succeeded by a Government of self-interest. What, for instance, can one think of Harding's latest declaration that American industry must be protected from competitors from a bankrupt Europe. How is Europe to pay its debts in that case?

A few days later Harding was elected President; "normalcy" became the watchword and the country settled down after a short bout of depression to the self-indulgent and debilitating decade that led up to the great crash of 1929.

CHAPTER 15

I Quit *The Times* for the Foreign Office

I JOINED F. in our London house, where everything was in order, furniture arranged, pictures hung, curtains up, servants installed. Paul was reported to be well and happy at school.

Next day came an infuriating shock. Steed asked me whether I would mind taking on the Paris correspondentship instead of the foreign editorship. Paris, he said, was the news center of the world. European reconstruction would depend upon Franco-British accord. *The Times* had had great influence on Anglo-French relations in the past and must have it again.

I told Steed that I should have to think things over, that I had left Washington to live in England, that, had I wanted to continue as a correspondent, I should never have dreamed of exchanging Washington for Paris or anywhere else. I asked him the reason for this inconsiderate treatment. Did he not know that I had taken a house in London? Northcliffe certainly did as he had gone over it with F. Surely he might have made up his mind that he did not after all need me in London in time to give me the choice between staying in Washington and moving to Paris. Steed weakly muttered something about financial stringency and his ability to be his own foreign editor.

It was an odious interview. The liking I had had for him was eclipsed by angry contempt.

Next, I went to Lints Smith, who had just become manager. He said that they had not written as they thought that I wanted to leave Washington because I had had enough of America and that, therefore, it would not much matter to me if I went to Paris instead of London. He added rather wryly that he would not mind being in a position to exchange London for Paris. I asked whether I should protest to Northcliffe. He said it would do no good as Northcliffe, who was becoming more and more difficult, had been thoroughly indoctrinated with the idea that Paris was the place where I could be most useful to *The Times*. He begged me to accept Paris.

I went home amazed that after our long and happy association *The Times* could treat me so scurvily. I told F. that I felt like resigning. She urged me not to be precipitate. Tyrrell next day suggested an explanation for my treatment. There had been a revolution in Printing House Square and I belonged to the ancien régime. I was too Dawsonian. My friendship with him and others at the Foreign Office would also be against me. He was deeply sorry that he had advised me to attempt the foreign editorship the year before but he had not then fully realized the situation in Printing House Square. As for Paris, he didn't know. The Foreign Office would like to have me there, but Paris was dangerously near to London, and the center of Steed's interest. So I could not expect the independence of Washington.

"Bill" Farrer, head of the law firm of his name and one of our closest friends, said that legally I was in a weak position as I had nothing in writing about my appointment. (There had been no question of written agreements or contracts so far as I was concerned under Northcliffe and Dawson.) He advised me not to resign as, if they could be made to withdraw the Paris offer, my claim for compensation would be less weak.

I saw Northcliffe, who took it for granted that I would go to Paris, and asked F. and me to come and stay with him in the country before we went there. The visit never came off. I never saw Northcliffe again. He passed completely out of my life until, after his death, I was informed of the legacy he had left me. I like to think that had he been his old self, I should have been differently treated. As for his subordinates, F.'s diary shows that the "top people" of *The Times* frequented our house during the first weeks of our negotiations.

For a time I was in some doubt whether I ought to master my indignation and go to France. A visit to Paris undertaken at the suggestion of *The Times* decided me. My task there I soon discovered would be downright disagreeable. In victory the French had found something tragically like defeat. Their mood was one of fear and resentment — fear of a vengeful Germany, resentment at the refusal of her late allies to appreciate the danger and provide the protection. Much controversy between Paris and London was inevitable. On each issue Steed would queer the case for Anglo-French unity by being too excitedly partisan. I discovered moreover that *The Times* no longer stood as high in Paris as it used to. I noted that:

> Diplomats and journalists consider *The Times* to be one of the most dangerous factors in Anglo-French relations. Our enemies in the Press here are continually using extracts from its leaders attacking our Government. Ronald Lindsay [then second-in-command at our embassy] said that the comment upon a news-sharing arrangement between Printing House Square and the *Petit Parisien* was "what a pity! the *Petit Parisien* used to be such a good friend of England."

On my return to London I was confronted by a generous contract. I haggled over it, and on March 7, 1921, F.'s diary contains the entry: "*The Times* withdraws Paris offer." I forget the details of what must have been a disagreeable discussion.

I do, however, recall very clearly the behavior of Lints Smith, with whom the negotiations must mainly have taken place. Nobody could have tried harder to make the intolerable tolerable. It was the beginning of a friendship that endured until his death. He gave me in the end what I thought was reasonable compensation, but afterward he told me that, had I been tough, I could have secured more. I did not, however, want to be tough. I owed far too much to *The Times* of the past to wish to exploit my grievance. What I wanted was a very long holiday. I did not get it.

A few days after I had become unemployed Tyrrell inquired about my plans. I told him that I had made up my mind never in any circumstances to tie myself up with any newspaper again. He asked me whether I would care to join the Foreign Office on a temporary basis to look after the American correspondents and to put my knowledge of America at its disposal as it was badly off in that respect, the head of the American department himself never having crossed the Atlantic. I demurred on the score of needing a rest. Tyrrell assured me that I should be anything but overworked. So F. and I abandoned our project of a summer on the Riviera.

I joined the Foreign Office in the spring of 1921, only to be hustled back to Washington almost at once. Both there and in London the high price of postwar government was being acutely felt. Large navies were costly; so why not reduce them? When the bogy of Anglo-American naval competition was raised at the Paris Peace Conference, Colonel House, I remembered, had told me not to worry, as "economic necessity" would make both sides see reason before long.

Where should the conference be held? Lloyd George wanted London and the chairmanship. The Foreign Office thought that the combination of London and the Prime Minister might be disastrous. As a leader in war the Prime Minister stood high in America. "Your Mr. Lloyd George sure does have a wonderful son," said the colored butler of a friend in New York, when the Prince of Wales was on his first visit to the United States. But as a politician he was regarded as the principal bamboozler of President Wilson.

There was also the American dislike of the Anglo-Japanese Alliance. Many in England, including the Prime Minister, liked it. But the Foreign Office thought that it would have to be scrapped if we were to get anywhere with the Americans. I said that that was also my impression and was told by Tyrrell to go over and make up my mind definitely.

I went with misgivings. The Ambassador, Sir Auckland Geddes, might reasonably resent the appearance of a minor Foreign Office emissary. Tyrrell said that I had means of securing information that a new ambassador could not possibly possess. Like his colleagues he disapproved of Geddes. The Prime Minister, with whom the Foreign Office was continually at odds, had had more than a finger in the appointment of this "outsider."

My misgivings were misplaced. Geddes was cordiality itself. He said that I must stay at the embassy as long as I liked. I returned to London after about a fortnight convinced that the Foreign Office was wrong about Geddes but right that the Japanese Alliance must be ended and that the conference must be in Washington. Lloyd George remained set upon London until President Harding came out for Washington. Whether he gave in then or later about the Japanese Alliance I do not remember.

The Washington announcement gave me a difficult day with my American newspapermen. Would Lloyd George or Lord Curzon, the Foreign Minister, lead our delegation? I could not admit that the Foreign Office rightly thought neither would do, that if the Prime Minister was too much mistrusted, the foreign minister was too pompous and out-of-date. I simply observed that the times were too busy for them to be so far and for so long away from home and that A. J. Balfour, whom Washington had liked so much in 1917, was the obvious man. For once the Foreign Office had its way and Balfour was appointed. Auckland Geddes and Lord Lee of Fareham, the First Lord of the Admiralty, were the other delegates. To me, more important than the delegates was Sir Maurice Hankey (afterward Lord Hankey), the secretary of the British and dominion delegations. I could not have done my work without him. He had held the same post at the Paris Peace Conference where I first met him. When at home he was secretary both to the Cabinet and the Committee of Imperial Defence and later on secretary of the Privy Council as well. He had been the key man behind the scenes in Whitehall during the war. I admired him unreservedly. He was smallish in stature. His face was rounded and firmly full, his forehead high, and his eyes sharp. He radiated health, energy, and quick intelligence and never seemed to tire. He was seldom seen in action without a battered official pouch bulging with papers out of which the right one appeared at the decisive moment. He and Tyrrell were the only senior officials I worked with who thoroughly understood what I was trying to do and that sending for journalists and lecturing them was a small and sometimes doubtful part of the game.

My assistant was Robert Wilberforce from our publicity office in New York, a great-great-grandson of his famous namesake. He was a good ally, quietly observant, outwardly nervous, inwardly tough, and liked by our clients. My secretary was Barbara Best. She had welcomed me to the office in that capacity and stayed with me until I left. She was a splendid assistant. She had considerable standing in the office. She was unflappable. Her memory was surprising. She knew the value of controlled indignation but was sparing in its use. My debt to her is immeasurable.

CHAPTER 16

A Showpiece of Anglo-American Cooperation

I SAILED FOR AMERICA in the *Olympic* toward the end of
October 1921. The ship swarmed with people bound for
the Washington Disarmament Conference. There were bands
of French, Chinese, Japanese, Italians, and Belgians. Srinivasa
Sastri, the Indian delegate, was on board, a most attractive
man who questioned me for hours about America. He had a
rather lovable secretary who, though no fool, was still bemused
by Oxford. His English was perfect, but his slang was twenty
years out of date. I thought that he resented us at the bottom
of his heart because he was not English.

Wickham Steed was another passenger. We met at Southampton on the gangway. He was wearing a cowboy hat. I wrote
to F., who had been left at home by illness: "Columbus on his
second voyage trying to live up to the aborigines." Steed knew
as little about America as he did about England and had lately
paid a rather unfortunate visit there with Northcliffe. He
greeted me effusively and I responded in kind. Curzon had
ordered the office to boycott *The Times* in a fit of autocratic
irascibility at its having rightly said that he would not do for
Washington, and here was a chance to close a breach that helped
nobody.

Lord Lee was on board. He had been a soldier before turning to politics. He had been attached to the American army in Cuba and was afterward military attaché in Washington. His wife, a rich and charming American, was with him. They had recently given Chequers to the nation to be a country house for prime ministers. Tyrrell had told me to teach him that an American wife and a friendship with Theodore Roosevelt were not the same thing as knowing the United States and to keep him from sailing off on the "Britannia rules the waves" tack. As a matter of fact Lee dealt with the press unprovocatively on landing and functioned inconspicuously at Washington, where Admiral Beatty got the limelight. The first time I met Beatty was at the Washington home of Mrs. Marshall Field, a millionaire relation of his wife's. I admired his good looks and exuberance and understood why he and Lord Lee did not get on. But I failed to realize until later how much he had helped the conference by discouraging a powerful group of senior American officers and their political friends from opposing naval reductions that he himself as a sailor cannot have much liked.

Our landing at New York was hectic: reporters, photographs, statements by Lee and Sastri, and no harm done. Robert Wilberforce greeted me. A special train to Washington, Italian carriage, Japanese carriage, Chinese carriage, British carriage, and some Belgians.

Hankey, who was to arrive a few days later with A. J. Balfour, had asked me to be ready with a report upon the Washington atmosphere. So I spent my first days in my old haunts. I was told that Congress was hotter than ever for retrenchment, that the Senate would ratify almost any agreement provided our Japanese treaty was abrogated and Japan was made to disgorge the parts of China she had stolen during the war. "But," said Senator McCormick and others, "the 'bamboozlement' of Woodrow Wilson isn't forgotten. So let it always appear that our people hold the initiative."

Then Maurice Peterson of the embassy, who was to be Balfour's secretary, and I set off to meet Balfour and Hankey and others at Quebec. We spent a day in New York. I lunched with Colonel and Mrs. House and had tea with the Franklin Roosevelts. I wrote to F.:

> Mrs. House, dear good soul, is the limit. I was telling House how Lloyd George had quarrelled with Henry Wilson. "Oh," said Mrs. House, "so he has quarrelled with President Wilson." "Not President Wilson, my dear, but the English Field Marshall Wilson," said the Colonel and then turning to me, "She would have gone and told a lot of women that Woodrow Wilson and Lloyd George had quarrelled, and the quarrel would have been dated back to the Peace Conference, and that is how stories start." After lunch House gave me a lot of stuff to pass on to Balfour.

Franklin Roosevelt was just back in his house from the hospital, after his attack of infantile paralysis. House feared that he would never be any good again. But Franklin himself was hopeful. He was getting the feel of his legs back.

Peterson and I took the night train for Montreal and changed there for Quebec next morning. Hitched onto the train was the private car of the Canadian Prime Minister, Arthur Meighen, who invited us to join him and I found myself caught up in the familiar machinery of transatlantic campaigning. Secretaries, reporters, drugstore port drunk out of lavatory glasses at midmorning, and finally the descent of the great man at a small station where the excitement was all the shriller for being in French. It was my first sight of inner Quebec and I was surprised to find it so American. Though voices and newspapers were French, the landscape was pure American, snake fences, frame houses, and all the rest. Even the advertisements looked American though they shouted French, and the inhabitants in their American-style clothes bore little resemblance to their cousins across the water. We met the Balfour party next morning. I suppose I must have arranged a press conference for Balfour. All I remember is a luxurious journey south in Canadian Pacific cars, much talk with Balfour, Hankey, and others. At Washington next morning there was a ceremonial descent from the train for which Peterson and I had taken tall hats to Quebec and back.

The first plenary session of the conference was on November 12, 1921, in the Hall of the Daughters of the American Revolution. Comparisons with the start of the Peace Conference were inevitable, and much to the advantage of Washington. The town was bright with autumn sunshine, whereas winter gloom had brooded over Paris. In Paris there was every prospect of endless trouble from inflamed nationalism; into the Hall of the Daughters of the Revolution we trooped in a mood of expectant good will.

President Harding opened the meeting in a colorless speech. He had a fine voice and presence but nothing else. Then came Charles E. Hughes, his secretary of state, with the most exciting speech that I was ever to hear at an international conference. Its key was the famous 5:5:3 ratio in battleships for the United States, Great Britain, and Japan. His bold eloquence surprised me. I had known him as a dignified, bearded guest at dinner parties in Washington while a member of the Supreme Court and as a colorless Republican candidate in the 1916 presidential election against Woodrow Wilson when Theodore Roosevelt had remarked that a razor could remove the difference from the two candidates in five minutes. Now, however, Hughes was in his element. His 5:5:3 proposal was quite unexpected. I had driven to the meeting with Balfour and Hankey. Balfour told us that when he had dined with Hughes the previous night he had not been given the slightest inkling of what the secretary of state was going to say.

The suggestion knocked everybody backward by its brutal simplicity. Beatty passed up to Balfour an obviously anxious note. Balfour, thin, stooping, distinguished, and benign, speaking, or rather thinking aloud, blessed Hughes' initiative without quite accepting it; this he did a few days later at the second plenary session after the necessary interchanges with London. Then came Briand, Prime Minister and Foreign Minister of France. Shouts for him began almost before the applause for A.J.B. ceased and produced a pathetic little incident. The old war-horse W. J. Bryan was sitting just behind me in the front row of the press seats, decrepit and neglected. He mistook the target of the shouts, half rose, and then sank back sadly.

The mellow richness of Briand's voice entranced even those who could not understand him. But the speech was thin. It was not France's day; it was not to be her conference. At the second plenary session Briand again missed fire. Out of his golden lips poured little but a catalogue of the grievances and fears of France. Disarmament was not mentioned; it was more important to keep armed against a renascent Germany:

> The French [I wrote to F. round about Christmas] are on everybody's nerves including their own. The Americans are irritated and even A.J.B., I think, went a little too far in his excoriation of them over submarines. [We wanted to abolish submarines; the French, and also the Americans, wanted to keep them.] Our people are stupid to abuse them. They will not realize that the more unpopular the French become, the more unpopular becomes Europe and the more remote the chance of American co-operation to put Europe on its economical feet . . .
>
> Yet I sympathise with them. They are still shocked by the war. The feeling that we and the United States let them down over the League and the treaties to protect them against Germany still rankles. With their congenital incapacity to grasp the point of view of the foreigner, they arrived here believing that they might still get those treaties and the cancellation of war debts out of the Conference. They find this impossible. They are left in the air with nothing to do while the Americans and British fraternise,

while the conference arranges capital ship ratios without consulting them, while outside the Conference they see the English mingling happily with Society. They are hedged around by alien speech. The other night at the Gridiron dinner to the Conference, A.J.B. answered for the allies and they were not called upon to speak . . .

After the second session, at which Balfour scored another triumph of informal eloquence, the conference settled down to three months of intensive and to me congenial work under English-speaking leadership. My task was twofold: to manage the press and to tell the delegation what I could about the opinions of Congress and the country.

For the first weeks I had Lord Riddell, owner of the *News of the World,* with me. He was a crony of Lloyd George's, his adviser on press matters, and had been his spokesman for the press at the Paris Peace Conference. I had attended one or two of his meetings and had admired the good-natured ability of his handling of questions. He had come to Washington because he thought the Prime Minister might suddenly decide to be there at first. The Foreign Office disapproved of him. I decided to make the best of him. Hankey agreed; it was arranged that he should take the daily press conferences that were expected of the delegation. Hankey, and any members of the delegation needed, briefed us after breakfast every day and we then went our own ways. I attended Riddell's press meeting when I could. The arrangement worked admirably.

The press adored him. They gave him a great banquet before he left all too soon. "Riddell goes this week," I wrote to F., "which will increase my work and diminish my amusement."

Riddell was not at all what one would expect the owner of the *News of the World* to be. His appearance was benignity itself. A surplice would have set well on him with his upright figure and white hair. In fact I think he did actually wear a surplice on one of the various occasions when he assisted Wilberforce and me to meet the stream of demands for speakers from the delegation. He had a dry sense of humor. He shrank from Washington society but I persuaded him to a dance at which I introduced him to a young girl. She gaped at him and exclaimed: "Are you a blood peer?" "No, miss," he replied, touching his forehead, "sweat of the brow, sweat of the brow."

After Riddell's departure I took the press conferences except when the ambassador had time to do so. Neither of us drew as big audiences as Riddell though the ambassador naturally beat me.

The naval treaty was signed in February 1922. Save in the case of submarines, the negotiations it involved did not worry me much. They were fairly open, or too technical to be newsworthy. Our failure to secure the abolition of submarines was not altogether to the bad. The pleasure it afforded them made the French more willing to go with us in the Far Eastern negotiations.

The importance of these negotiations lay in the possibility first that unless the Japanese agreed to quit China, the Senate might refuse to ratify the naval treaty in spite of our having scrapped the Anglo-Japanese Alliance, and secondly that, unless the Japanese were reassured as to the continuation of their membership of the club of the Great Powers given them by our alliance, they might refuse to play. Hence the first of the treaties completed was the Four-Power Treaty signed by the United States, Great Britain, France, and Japan to protect peace and promote order in the Far East. It gave the Japanese their equality.

Getting the Japanese out of China was a more difficult exercise. It involved very delicate direct negotiation between the Japanese and the Chinese, each thoroughly antipathetic to the other. Out of this inauspicious confrontation, Hughes and

Balfour, working harmoniously and patiently, produced the Shantung Treaty, of which the first clause restored the German-leased territory of Kiaochow to China. I was fascinated by this exercise in diplomacy in which I played a small part as an alleged authority on the mood of the Senate. It was such a mixture of blandishment and blackmail. It did not, however, have its desired effect. China remained in a state of aggravating confusion, and ten years later the Japanese were again plundering her and the other cosignatories and the League of Nations was registering impotent protestations with varying degrees of sincerity.

The only break I had in our three months in Washington was a couple of nights in New York where Balfour addressed an English-Speaking Union dinner about a thousand strong. He, Peterson, and I stayed with Mrs. Whitelaw Reid, a generous Park Lane hostess in London when her husband was ambassador, and now equally lavish in New York. "How do you like Palace Life, Willert?" A.J.B. whispered to me over the sideboard at breakfast. He was at his best on that expedition. On our way back from the E.S.U. dinner we went round by Broadway and Times Square to show him the lights. They did not interest him. His attention went to the motley multiracial swarm upon the sidewalks. He told our driver to slow down. He wanted to get out and walk back to Mrs. Reid's near St. Patrick's Cathedral. The obvious objections prevailed. It was surprising to find a man so aloof and fastidious wishing to rub shoulders with a mob of which each individual component would be utterly distasteful to him. But racial and national experiments attracted him: Zionism on a small scale, the United States on a vast scale, and here was an opportunity of seeing the American "melting pot" in action.

Balfour was wonderfully tireless for his seventy-three years. After strenuous days of negotiation he was often to be seen at parties, alert and courteously interested in his interlocutors. As I have already said, he was the sole foreign speaker at the dinner of the Gridiron Club just before Christmas:

> We sat down at 7.45 [I wrote to F.] and it was midnight before we got to coffee. Interminable waits between courses filled in with stunts and speeches. The President and Cabinet, of course, and all the delegates were among the 450 diners. Hughes, Taft, A.J.B. and the President spoke. Hughes was stilted but witty, Taft genial and amusing, A.J.B. serious and graceful, Harding serious and pathetically childish. They had rotted him about "normalcy" and he tried to explain what it meant. Apparently it means an individualistic Utopia espied through glasses clouded by the nebulous sentimentalism of the Middle West.

I came away from the entertainment with A.J.B. wondering whether I should be as fresh as he was, at his age, after a similar ordeal.

Balfour's success throughout the conference more than compensated for the failure of the French. It turned the American eye back toward Europe to a certain extent. By the end of the year Hughes felt able to make a once famous speech pointing out that Europe's economic problems were also America's, and the first step had been taken toward American participation in the series of efforts, of which the Dawes plan stood out, to settle German reparations.

CHAPTER 17

The Foreign Office in the 1920s —
The Locarno Myth

ON MY RETURN TO LONDON, Tyrrell asked me whether I would take on the whole of the press, which, except for the Americans, was being dealt with by the private secretary of the foreign minister. It was some years, however, before the rest of the publicity machine was in my hands and the News Department was consolidated into a real department. Long afterward, when he was ambassador in Paris, Tyrrell told me that he had always meant this to happen, but that he had had to move slowly owing to prejudice against the innovation.

My first months were leisurely and I had time to look around me. Tensions on the Rhine and further east occasionally brought a superfluity of journalists to see us, but usually the bulk of our visitors were regular callers seeking background as much as hot news. It was, as Tyrrell said it would be, a welcome rest after Washington. I found it fascinating to be inside a great government office with which I had had so much to do from the outside. Also it was changing as *The Times* had to change more roughly when Northcliffe took it over. In both cases a comfortable but outdated exclusiveness was vanishing, though very slowly in the Foreign Office. There was still an atmosphere of exclusiveness and privilege about it. It looked down upon other government departments, with the exception of the Treasury. In the higher ranks there was a tendency toward professional exclusiveness — unnecessary secrecy, private letters instead of official dispatches, a handicap to historians of the future and to press officers of the present, for without full and accurate information a press officer is a guideless traveler in a dangerous jungle. New ideas, like the League of Nations or potential American world supremacy, provoked suspicion rather than sympathetic curiosity.

I was by no means the only outsider to be admitted in those postwar years. But the Office was still infinitesimal as compared with its successor of today. In the 1925 list, the permanent undersecretary had a deputy and two assistant undersecretaries, the foreign minister had a private secretary with a couple of assistants. There were only eight political departments for me to keep in touch with, possessing a combined membership of forty-eight. Parliament was represented only by the secretary of state and his parliamentary undersecretary. Thus one soon knew everyone. Of the various friends I found there my old schoolfellow Robert Vansittart, Curzon's private secretary, was the most important. He was most helpful to me in finding my feet. So, of course, was Tyrrell. Tyrrell was then second-in-command of the office. His chief, the permanent undersecretary, was Sir Eyre Crowe, a diplomat of the old school and one of the finest characters that I have come across in my long life.

Crowe was almost a recluse. His appearances in the great world were as infrequent as he could make them. The office, lunch at his club, and home for dinner often at some ungodly hour was his routine. Through his mother he had German blood. But he had no illusions about the Germany that Bismarck had created. A memorandum about her danger written in 1907 is one of the great state papers of the period. The politicians, of course, ignored him as Neville Chamberlain and his appeasers ignored his successor, Vansittart, a generation later and with the same terrible result. Crowe never hid from me his contempt of politicians. He sent for me one morning and pointed an accusing finger at something in some newspaper that ought not to have been there. "How do you think that got out?" he asked. "It has been circulated to the Cabinet," I said. "My dear fellow, I apologise for my base suspicions," he replied.

A day or two after I arrived at the Office, Crowe asked me out to lunch. He said that he could not see why I was necessary, why diplomacy had to hold the press in such consideration. But Tyrrell, who knew about these things, said it was. Therefore he, Crowe, would always be at my disposal. And this he was, frank, patient, kindly, and illuminating. He was a good administrator, though inclined to pay too much attention to details. There was in my time a frame hung somewhere in the office containing a minute of his that ordered the use of string tags for the securing of papers together, the tags to be inserted exactly one inch from the left-hand top corner of the sheaf, as shown in the minute. Metal clips were forbidden as apt to catch up together discordant papers.

Crowe died in 1925 and Tyrrell succeeded him. Tyrrell was the opposite of Crowe; one wondered how they worked so well together. He went everywhere and knew everybody. Crowe never entered our house; Tyrrell was frequently there and we in his. He was an accomplished and informative conversationalist. He was, as I had every reason to know, a very good friend but he could also be a bad enemy. He was accessible and easygoing in the office and hated putting himself on paper at any length. Many thought him lazy. Once when we were crossing St. James's Park he suddenly said: "They think me lazy in the Office, don't they?" I cannot recall how I dealt with this poser, but I remember his answer: "Can't they see that my job is to sit on the fence for nine days and come down on the right side on the tenth?"

Another good ally of mind and the outstanding oddity of the Office was Stephen Gaselee, its librarian. We had the same tutor at Eton where he was a colleger and a brilliant scholar. Even at school, where conformity ruled, he wore red socks and red mittens. In later life I saw him in an April sleet shower on the Horse Guards Parade dressed in a broadcloth tailcoat with pockets at the sides, white duck trousers, tall hat, and an old Etonian tie tied in a bow. He loved good food and wine and conversation. He told me once that he had for years break-fasted on anchovies, dry toast, and black coffee. He called himself a High Tory, cultivated friendships with minor royalties, snort with black powder, and died too young.

Our next greatest oddity in my first year was Lord Curzon, the Secretary of State. The difference was that Gaselee had deliberately placed himself in another century, whereas nature had done it for Curzon. He was both formidable and ridiculous. A good and well-stored mind was distorted by kinks and prejudices, tremendous industry compromised by unessential activities such as handwritten communications that might just as well have been dictated. He was sensitive to the press, which meant spasms of trouble for me. There were occasional exceptions when I was patted on the back. On one such he excelled himself. As I left his room, I said that I hoped that appreciation this time would not be followed by the reverse next time. "My dear Willert, if you praise your butler for the state of your plate, there is a scratch on your best salver next day; if you praise a housemaid for the way in which she keeps your china, crash! and a bit of your best piece of Sèvres has gone. But let us leave superstition of that sort to that class."

He had, however, a sense of humor. I once persuaded him to accept an invitation to a press lunch and escorted him to it. To my surprise he kept his critical audience well amused. The press, he said, among other jibes at it, had sometimes been unfair to him. There was a murmur of protest — "Yes," he retorted, "and here is an example. When I was Viceroy of India you may remember there was a Durbar. The King came out to it. He did me the honour of asking me to draft his speech. My draft was accepted without alteration. The Durbar took place. Next day the press compared the clear manly delivery of the monarch with the turgid rhetoric of the Viceroy. Now, I ask you, was that fair?"

Curzon could be vague about the identity of subordinates. One of the departmental heads — and as I have said there were not many of them — ran into him in Paddington Station, relieved him of a bag, and put him into the appropriate compartment. "It may interest you to know," said the marquis, "that you have carried the bag of Lord Curzon." His pomposity would occasionally desert him. One morning he was stuck in the private lift to his room for some time with his chin level with the floor. In the afternoon I ran into the head office keeper. "You must," I said, "have had a tough morning." "Yes, sir," he replied, "but it was repaying. I thought that, after my time in the army, I knew everything about bad language. I found I was wrong."

"It's odd that we should have had to wait for the Labour Party to give us a gentleman," said Alec Cadogan, a fastidious man, as a group of us left Ramsay MacDonald's room after our first meeting with him when he took office in 1924 as both Prime Minister and foreign secretary in the first Labour government. The wooliness that afflicted him at times in his second premiership was then entirely absent. He knew what he wanted and considering the short time he was in office secured a good deal of it. He also, to my joy, knew that the press and its management had a place in diplomacy. He sent for me after a day or two to tell me his main objectives. They were good relations with France, which would make it easier to bring Germany back into the European family, less bad relations with Russia, and a strong League of Nations well buttressed by Britain. He asked me to make the press understand that it was more difficult for Labour to deal with the Kremlin than for the Conservatives, as the Russians regard British Labour as renegades, as deserters to the bourgeoisie. With the Russians, Ramsay succeeded in negotiating a trade treaty that failed, though not through any fault of his diplomacy, to take effect.

With France he was successful — up to a point. Curzon had not been able to do much with her. Lloyd George was in the way and he failed to hit it off with their tough and able little Prime Minister, Raymond Poincaré, who had occupied the Ruhr because the Germans were defaulting on reparations. MacDonald was determined to stop this and was favored by the fact that the reparations commission under the American, General Dawes, had just put in a constructive report that needed acceptance by an international conference, the first at which the Germans and the French would meet since the war. He wrote to Poincaré a human and friendly letter. He pointed out that England had, in her areas of unemployment, her devastated districts as well as France.

Poincaré responded in kind, but before the conference could be held he was succeeded by Herriot, like MacDonald, a socialist. That made the conference easier and it afforded an example of MacDonald at his best. It was a small affair held in the secretary of state's room at the Foreign Office. The Germans were only summoned at the last moment. One could feel the strain as we awaited their entry. The Prime Minister was presiding at the end of the table away from the door. He whispered to Hankey to receive the Germans at the door and bring them to him. He introduced them to the French. A smiling conversation broke the tension. The Dawes plan was accepted and the Germans paid up more or less until a few months before Hitler's accession, though for most of that time they were also rearming surreptitiously and illegally.

MacDonald attended the 1924 assembly of the League of Nations. He was the first British Prime Minister or foreign minister to do so. Having settled reparations he was more anxious than ever to straighten out the tortured affairs of the world, which still meant Europe to a far greater extent than now. He was in that respect a warm-hearted Woodrow Wilson. I once overheard him remark, in his Scottish accent, when starting on a before-breakfast stroll at Geneva: "What I always say is: 'Before breakfast for myself and the rest of the day for the world!' " He negotiated the Geneva Protocol, which, very roughly, made us part of the police force of Europe instead of limiting our direct responsibilities to the Rhine and westward as Locarno soon did.

The Protocol, like the Russian trade treaty, came to nothing. Two fortuitous incidents, the Campbell case and the Zinoviev letter, blew Labour out of office before the end of 1924.

Stanley Baldwin and the Conservatives stayed in office till 1929 with Austen Chamberlain as foreign minister. Those were dull years for me. Europe seemed to be settling down. Austen Chamberlain was anything but news-conscious. He was the kindest and most considerate of men, a first-class human being but a second-class foreign minister. His imagination did not stretch far enough for my needs. Our personal relations were nevertheless excellent. At the end of his term he wrote me a note asking me not to lose touch with him and ending with: "It was your business to be importunate on occasions, but I hope that, if I sometimes showed a little impatience, you did not misunderstand it or suspect me of any lack of appreciation of the help you were giving me."

An outstanding example of his ignorance of the needs of those who deal with the news of international politics was afforded by the signature of the Locarno Pact in the Foreign Office in 1925. It was the great event of Chamberlain's foreign secretaryship. I knew that the press from all over Europe were coming to witness it and asked Chamberlain about arrangements. He said categorically that he meant to have the ceremony in dignified privacy. I protested and argued in vain, reminding him of all the press had done to popularize the "spirit of Locarno," etc., etc. I appealed to Tyrrell. He, of course, sympathized and sent me on to the Prime Minister. Baldwin was notoriously indifferent to foreign affairs. But he was not indifferent to public opinion, and it did not take much persuasion to cause him to intervene, and the press were admitted to the signature. But I had to arrange for them to come in by a back way so as not to compromise the dignity of the proceedings by their mixing with the signatories.

The Locarno agreement was built upon the grave of the Labour Party's Protocol. I went with Chamberlain to Geneva for the funeral of the Protocol. It was hardly a British press officer's holiday. The repudiation of the Protocol was bitterly resented by League enthusiasts. I recall Chamberlain saying to me on our way home that something would have to be done to comfort them. Hence the Locarno agreement. The agreement fortified peace on the Rhine but did little to help the League of Nations to prevent war in Eastern and Central Europe. Yet it was widely welcomed as a long step toward lasting peace and did help to give Europe some years of deceptive comfort. My own opinion of it I can best convey by a couple of extracts from a series of lectures I gave to the American

Institute of Politics at Williamstown in Massachusetts in 1927, when the European euphoria was at its height. They were afterward published as a small book by Yale University Press. The quotation comes from a chapter entitled "Peace without Security":

> It was recognised in Britain that with the stability of Western Europe, British interests were inextricably involved; but in spite of the fact that the Great War had come out of the centre of the continent, it was not realized that in the last analysis political Europe is one and indivisible and that an armed infraction of the Polish frontier would lead inevitably to war on the Rhine and would thus implicate Western Europe . . .
>
> Its [Locarno's] value is, when all is said and done, chiefly psychological. By suddenly and dramatically fulfilling hope too long deferred it has given Europe a much needed breathing time, a much needed sedative.

I should have liked to go further. But as a member of the Foreign Office I obviously could not. My position, indeed, was rather anomalous and a good example of Tyrrell's practical nonconformity. The other two lecturers were Peter Reinhold, the Minister of Finance in the Weimar government, and Count Carlo Sforza, the distinguished Italian diplomat and opponent of Mussolini. From England they had wanted Lord Eustace Percy. He, however, as president of the Board of Education, was too busy to accept and suggested me as a substitute.

The expedition was an agreeable change from officialdom. F. and Paul went with me. We paid a visit to the Franklin Roosevelts at Hyde Park. He was supporting Al Smith in his unsuccessful bid for the presidency against Herbert Hoover. About my only clear memory of some quiet and pleasant days was a discussion of the job he would take if Smith won. Why not the London Embassy, I asked. "I should like it," he said, "but a post involving a lot of ceremonial is impossible for me."

As a matter of fact he told me, when President, that his disability was not all to the bad. "I can shelter myself behind it quite a lot." After a short stay in Washington, a few days in New York where we had our information center, the British Library of Information, which comes under the News Department; then some visits in New England and home, via Montreal.

Back in the Foreign Office life was uneventful until in 1929 Labour took hold again and the American panic of that year promised a quickening of the European pulse.

CHAPTER 18

British Labour Vitalizes the League

THIS TIME — in 1929 — Ramsay MacDonald contented himself with the premiership and gave the Foreign Office to Arthur Henderson. Of all my political chiefs Henderson was the one I liked best. There was no pretense about him. He was at once wise and simple. As Alec Cadogan who served him at Geneva said, he was the sort of man one would go to in private trouble. He was soon affectionately known in the office and in the corridors of Geneva as "Uncle Arthur."

Like MacDonald, but unlike most of my official colleagues with the exception of Tyrrell, Henderson understood how to use the press. It was natural that the two chief architects of a popular party should do so. Hugh Dalton, Henderson's parliamentary undersecretary, was equally cooperative. He was not a popular man. He was rather overwhelming. He was large, he bent over one; his eyes pierced and his voice boomed. But we got on well together. When the Labour Party exploded in 1931 and he went out of office, F. and I would sometimes motor over from Oxford, on the outskirts of which I had taken over the house in which I was born, and spend the day with him and his wife, who was a member of the London County Council, at their cottage in Wiltshire.

Henderson sent for me a few days after his arrival. He cross-questioned me about the personnel and working of the News Department. He stressed the importance he attached to it. He said that I should find him more practical than MacDonald. MacDonald had put his money on the Protocol. The Conservatives had destroyed it. Henderson was betting upon the Disarmament Conference, preparations for which had been going on in Geneva for some time. He told me to keep in very close touch with himself and Dalton as he foresaw occasions when their views and those of the Office might not coincide.

This I interpreted as due to two causes: first, that the Foreign Office as a whole never really believed in the League, and secondly, the lack of sympathy between Henderson and MacDonald. MacDonald, for instance, promoted Vansittart to be head of the Foreign Office over the heads of several people whom Henderson would have preferred. Gossip had it that this was to keep a hidden control over the Foreign Office. I never believed it. In my experience, Van worked loyally with his chief, and, wholly different though their personalities were, they agreed about the German danger, though their plans for meeting it were not identical.

After Crowe and Tyrrell, Vansittart was the most remarkable personality in the Office in my time. Like them he became its head. Unlike them, in spite of his brilliance, he must be written down as a failure. He calls himself so in the curiously but characteristically involved memoirs that his premature death left unfinished. His principal aim when he became head was to persuade the politicians to prepare for war against Germany. He failed partly because people like Neville Chamberlain, John Simon, and Samuel Hoare were, as I too discovered with Simon at Geneva, impervious to European realities and partly because he was not the man for the job. His literary brilliance enabled him to produce in Paris, in French,

a play while he was still an attaché at the Paris Embassy that ran
for some months, but not the simply marshaled argument of a
Crowe that politicians could understand. I remember finding
myself at lunch at the club one Monday next to a friend from
another department. I asked him how he had been spending
the weekend. "Translating one of Van's papers into English
for my master," he replied.

Vansittart lacked, too, the common touch. He was principally responsible for the Hoare-Laval Agreement indignation,
opposition to which blew Samuel Hoare out of the Foreign
Office. He gave Hitler's propagandist, Goebbels, a grand
present when it leaked out that he was arguing that Germany
should be "kept lean." He was not a real League of Nations
man. He never, so far as I remember, came out squarely for
collective security, for to put it in the old diplomatic terms,
such a marshaling of the peace-loving countries that Germany
might not have dared to bluff her way into war. I suggested to
him more than once that he should resign and join the League
of Nations people for he was a good speaker. He answered that
civil servants do not resign and continued to do his bit by minutes, which the politicians ignored, and by supplying Winston
Churchill with ammunition.

Later when I had my row with Simon, or rather he with me,
and departed, I did not ask for his support and did not get
it. I wanted neither to stay in the Office nor to embarrass him.
We had been good friends in the Office and also at Eton where
he had a scintillating career in both work and games. He won,
among other things, both the French and German prizes, a
"double" that had not been brought off by anybody but my
father, at the time, to the best of my knowledge.

Arthur Henderson was first and foremost a believer in the
League. He saw its effective use and strengthening as the best
safeguard of peace and that a successful disarmament con-

ference was the best means to that end. MacDonald's thoughts ran on the same lines, though more mistily. He had been a pacifist during the war; Henderson a member of the War Cabinet. He and Dalton both realized the potential menace of Germany and had a deeper sympathy with French nervousness than Mac-Donald. Henderson and MacDonald were opposites in many ways. MacDonald liked high society. Henderson was content with his humble origins. He was a solid nonconformist. Two typical passages with him come to mind. The first was in the train between Geneva and Calais. He suddenly asked me to "Go to the restaurant car and get me a large glass, half port, half brandy." I must have shown surprise at such a request for so strong a teetotaler. "Yes," he said, "that is what we always used against the collywobbles on the Tyne-side." Once, just before Christmas, I minuted that some paper could be dealt with "after Xmas." It was returned to me with a reprimand for not writing the holy word in full. To Henderson, also, I was personally indebted. To him, together with Vansittart and Warren Fisher, the head of the Civil Service, I owed a promotion to the status, and salary, but not the title of assistant undersecretary.

Arthur Henderson soon asserted himself in the office and in Parliament. In the office he settled a long controversy over policy and personalities in Egypt in a liberal fashion. In Parliament he triumphed in regard to the "optional clause." The "optional clause," forgotten now, was important then. It was an agreement extending the scope of arbitration. The Conservatives thought it went too far, but after a tough debate Henderson was authorized to sign it unchanged at the autumn session of the League assembly.

Soon after the debate Dalton told me that I must come to Geneva for the autumn council and the annual assembly and bring an assistant. The Prime Minister, the secretary of state, and Lord Robert Cecil would all be there and the string of experts must be equally strong. Lord Robert (afterward Lord Cecil of Chelwood) in politics and Gilbert Murray outside it were the leaders of the League of Nations movement in England.

It was a very different assembly from the last one I had attended at which Austen Chamberlain had repudiated the Protocol. Then the British role was distasteful and depressing; now it was popular and hopeful. There were dreams of the League becoming, under British and French leadership and with the blessing of America, a sort of United Europe, for its membership was still mainly European.

Henderson soon dominated. His star turn was the signature of the "optional clause." It took place in the temporary League building in which I had stayed as a hotel when I was at Oxford. The room was crowded and motionless, save for a swirl of photographers around the signatories. Henderson handled his pen with slow self-possession, red in the face from suppressed emotion. At our press conference afterward he glowed with satisfaction; the murder of the Protocol had been avenged. It was during those days that I began to really know and love "Uncle Arthur."

I also learned a lot about Geneva. I was not hard-pressed; no controversial questions came up. Everything was in the open, including some flattering jealousy of the position our representatives were making for themselves. I had time to foster friendships among the secretariat of the League and newspaper correspondents invaluable to me later on. F. and I explored the agreeable surroundings of the town, the little villages on the lake and inland, the Jura and other neighboring mountains, for then as always we had our car with us.

Back in London I transferred my allegiance temporarily to the Prime Minister who, in those days, had no press officer.

The third Naval Disarmament Conference under his presidency came on almost at once. The second conference had failed in Geneva in 1927, when I was in America, partly owing to the bad handling of the press. I was determined that if anything went wrong this time it should not be the fault of the press arrangements. My first step was to demand and, thanks to the support of Maurice Hankey, to secure about as much floor space for the press as was planned for the conference itself, for which St. James's Palace was being prepared.

Adapting part of a Tudor building for the press needs of a large conference was quite a problem, or would have been had not the technicians of the post office and the office of works tackled it with helpful enthusiasm. An article in the *World Press News* reminds me of some of the things they did. There was a post office that provided anything from a postal order to an apparatus for telegraphing photographs; there were fifty-two telephone booths, half of which were connected with press agencies or newspaper offices; and there was some special arrangement to speed up continental telephone calls. The only thing I failed to secure was an alcoholic bar.

> Since I criticised the handling of the press at the Geneva Naval Conference with some severity [wrote J. A. Spender, the grand old man of London journalism in the *Daily News*], I should like to be among the first to say that its handling at the present conference has been above reproach. By common consent Sir Arthur Willert has done a difficult piece of work with admirable skill and tact . . .

The Prime Minister was really responsible for the success of our publicity. He was back at his best and he was a born showman. He got the King to welcome the meeting in a broadcast speech at the House of Lords. The mayor of London was persuaded to give a Guildhall banquet; other functions were arranged. He was excellent with the press. He was always willing to see journalists separately or together. He let me bring

parties of them to Chequers. One foreign party I remember
vividly. It was a bitter February east wind day. After showing the house he insisted on taking the group, on foot, to a
nearby knob of the Chilterns, where one was supposed to see
I forget how many counties. "Here," he said, "is where a Prime
Minister of England can receive his inspiration." The thinly
clad group shivered and gazed.

I had to arrange for photographs at every opportunity. Some
of them have survived. They go all the way from the King
making his wireless speech to me displaying the signed treaty.
The Prime Minister collected the delegates on a bleak winter
morning in the garden of 10, Downing Street for broadcast-
ing and photography. I had felt myself an integral and hard-
worked satellite of that conference and it pleased me as we
left Downing Street that morning to overhear Stimson, the
American Secretary of State, tell MacDonald that he wished
the State Department had somebody like me! It was satisfactory, too, to have participated in another successful conference, though subsequent events brought it to nothing.

CHAPTER 19

British Conservatism Kills the League

S UCCESS IN LONDON was speedily obliterated at Geneva. The big Disarmament Conference from which so much was expected opened there in February 1932. Two years later it was petering out in disastrous failure. Europe had been handed over to Hitler, though then and for some time afterward one hoped that war might still be avoided.

But only if Britain gave the leadership. Hitler had to be shown that the series of brutal bluffs like the grabbing of Austria and Czechoslovakia would inevitably end in banding the peace-loving countries against him in arms. The French saw this from the first. The main issue of the Disarmament Conference was, though I doubt whether the phrase had yet been invented, "collective security." The French spokesman at the opening session of the conference came out for an international army. He was André Tardieu, then Prime Minister. He told me at the time that the main issue of the conference would be the reconciliation of the German demand for equality with the French need for safety. This would only be obtained if Britain would come into Europe and join France at the head of a grand alliance between the peace-loving countries, which would reinforce the League as guardian of the peace and show Germany that armed diplomacy, wherever practiced, could not succeed. Britain shirked the issue.

She shirked it because the Conservatives, Locarno-minded people, were to all intents and purposes back in power. The Labour government, broken by the financial crisis of 1931, had been succeeded by a coalition. Ramsay MacDonald remained Prime Minister, but the Conservatives controlled Arthur Henderson and most of the Labour Party had gone into bitter opposition. In their place MacDonald received the support of a group of Liberals (National Liberals they called themselves) of whom Sir John Simon, a lawyer who had made his mark on contemporary domestic history and in the law courts, was the leader. MacDonald made him foreign minister. A worse appointment could not have been conceived. His outlook on Europe lacked both knowledge and conviction, and tact was not his strong point.

The conference started under the worst of auspices. Simon had no welcome for Tardieu's suggestion. His speech was cold and unconstructive. He told me before we left London that all we were prepared to do was to support anyone with a practical plan. Arthur Henderson, chosen by acclamation as president of the conference in the heyday of his popularity, was now out of office, out of Parliament, and in bad health. His health improved later on. But he was not on speaking terms with MacDonald and hardly with Simon. His personal popularity with the League secretariat and the powerful corps of newspaper correspondents hurt rather than helped the British official position and especially that of Simon.

So did the Japanese rape of Manchuria and their attack upon Shanghai, then in full progress. Both were international illegalities of the first water. But the British conservative "establishment" rather sympathized with them for the indisputable reason that the Chinese had been quite impossible to deal with since the Washington Conference. The League secretariat and the majority of the press people at Geneva took the other line. If Japan were allowed to ride roughshod over the Covenant, Germany, with Hitler well above the horizon and known to be surreptitiously rearming harder than ever, would be encouraged to intensify his power politics, and so might Mussolini with all his vaporing about the revival of the power of imperial Rome. It was very clear to Wilberforce (who had again joined me from New York) and myself that this was going to be for us a much more difficult conference than Washington.

Simon soon justified our apprehensions. It was at a lunch given him by the American and British correspondents — a formidable band. On our way to it I urged him not to say anything that would increase the impression that we were pro-Japanese, which was damaging us a lot. What happened is best related by an excerpt from my diary (subsequent quotations in this chapter come from the same source). Simon said that:

> The Japanese deserved sympathy as they were only doing what we had done in the past, i.e. seeking means for necessary expansion. This tactlessness, which the Secretary of State was the first to admit, has made a rotten impression. The speech was "off the record"; but this amazing remark was inevitably and quickly everybody's property.

Simon was never able to adapt himself to a cosmopolitan audience. He was equally unable to assess the psychology of foreign countries (he was afterward Neville Chamberlain's chief supporter over "appeasement") and was also uncomfortably placed at Geneva. MacDonald was too much preoccupied to be there much. He only came out on flying visits, usually and often successfully to break a deadlock. And though Simon served him loyally on those occasions, it cannot have increased his self-confidence to have the Prime Minister succeeding where he had failed. I used to feel indeed that one of the causes of Simon's failure was lack of self-confidence. He once said to me that he wished he was "not such a cold-blooded fish." He also, I thought, was more sensitive than the Prime Minister about being in Conservative chains. "What," he said to me when I suggested a liberal solution of some problem, "and have all those Tories on my back."

Once in London when I was accompanying him to some press function he was obviously nervous about his speech and told me that this was always the case when he had to speak outside the law courts. Certainly at Geneva I only once saw him happy and successful. That was when the Council of the League was acting as a law court and he as advocate of the Anglo-Persian Oil Company against the Persian government. I sat with him while he picked the brains of the magnates of the company and when he put his case together afterward. I listened to its brilliant presentation next day. When I congratulated him he said: "It was easy; so easy that I was afraid I had gone too far. Doing too well is a lawyer's trap."

His speeches during that February and March session of 1932 were disastrous. Neither the Prime Minister nor any other prominent member of the delegation came out to help him. Here is an extract from my diary to show what his press officers were up against:

A heavy afternoon and evening yesterday over the Secretary of State's speech to the Assembly on the Sino-Japanese affair. The substance of the speech was good . . . But its manner was bad — gestures, intonation, stressing of words in such a way as often to obscure the meaning of simple sentences. The press gallery grinned and hummed afterwards with ribald remarks about physical exercises in public, etc. etc. More serious is the effect of insincerity which the elaborate manner apparently gives. Blankenstein [a Dutch journalist who counted] asked why, if we cannot avoid producing them, we don't keep such Englishmen at home. W.N. Ewer [the able correspondent of the *Daily Herald* and a very good friend to me] said that he never thought that the time could come when, as an Englishman, he would wish to see Austen Chamberlain, of whom he had been a bitter critic, back in Geneva.

At the end of the winter session I had this to say:

We have not had a good press though the S. of S. has been let off lightly when one compares what has been said about him with what has been written about him. It is hardly surprising that we should be thought uninterested in the conference when we have never had a full delegation here.

Lest it may seem that the quick slump in British stock was confined to the press, I will add two comments from other sources during the same period:

One of the American delegates, Senator Swanson, an old Washington friend, unburdened himself to me the other evening as follows:

England's prestige had slumped distressingly. He hoped and believed that the slump would only be temporary. England was a decent country. She was a hundred per cent — at least eighty per cent — honest and the world needed her . . .

Erik Colban, Norwegian delegate and like the Senator a friendly observer [afterward he was minister in London], said that it "does not matter who is French Foreign Minister as France has a Foreign policy: England has none". Out of the Far Eastern business too, he prophesised we "should come with shame".

After Easter the Prime Minister and American Secretary of State Stimson attended. The Americans produced a plan. The conference brightened but not for long. Strong British support for the American plan was lacking. I think it must have been after Simon's speech in support of it that Hugh Gibson, the American delegate, made his remark about "praising with faint damns." The Germans left the Conference on the ground that not enough was being done to give them "equality" and it went into a depressing summer recess.

We met again in the autumn in what I called the worst of circumstances:

> Germany and France are on each other's nerves, the one talking about rearming, the other about the inevitability of war. The Conference lacks a programme and our Government lacks a policy. Everybody looks to us for a lead and we refuse to look the situation in the face.

Ineffectiveness continued until just before Christmas when MacDonald swooped down on the Conference and cleverly persuaded the Germans back into it. In the spring we produced a British plan. But it was not good enough for Hitler, who had gained power the previous January (1933). In the autumn Simon reintroduced the plan, amended in the interests of Germany. Hopes ran high. Immense pains were taken to sugar Simon's speech to Hitler's taste. The speech was quite well received by the Germans who heard it. F. and I went off to a Lucullan lunch at Maurice de Rothschild's villa. We had a rough return to reality. A member of the League secretariat stopped us to say that Hitler had refused our offer. I asked Simon whether he would like to see the press. No, he wouldn't; the press had done him enough harm already. Nothing was said about my management of it but the implication of bitter reproach was clear. Disappointment at Hitler's attitude, realization that it probably meant the failure of the conference and consequently a heavy blow to his prestige, had knocked the secretary of state off his balance.

He made this clear next day. There had been some muddle about the reporting of his speech at home for which neither I nor Wilberforce had the slightest responsibility. But I was told among other things that:

> I was too old for my job. What he wanted was some young man who could interpret his mind and pass it on to the press in the right way. I retorted that my trouble was not age but ignorance.

He was giving me no private guidance and he had failed to ask me to his recent policy discussions. He snarled that my desire to attend these discussions was "mere idle curiosity". I said that that was "about the unfairest thing ever said to me".

What my diary calls "some comic relief" was then given to a strained situation: the secretary of state suddenly seized the telephone and crying, "I will give you a lesson in your own work," got the news editor of *The Times* and gave him a lecture. No trace of it appeared in the next day's paper for, as Dawson told me afterward, Simon seemed to his interlocutor to be in a "very strange state of mind." Other equally unpleasant interviews followed into two of which Simon was ill-advised enough to bring two highly respected members of the press corps.

I ought to have resigned on the spot. I had never been entirely happy in the Foreign Office even when Tyrrell and Arthur Henderson were there. Journalism was in my blood. The financial depression of the 1930s would make welcome the increase of income I knew I could make free-lancing and perhaps book-writing. British foreign policy was easier to attack than to defend and explain, etc., etc. Why did I not then quit? Partly at first because I had a feeling not entirely unrelated to pity for Simon. He was so obviously and so vulnerably the wrong man in the wrong place. He was about as much at home in Geneva as a small-town English solicitor would be if suddenly plunged into a complicated "big business" case in Chicago. As I have related, his only success was when he had to play the lawyer. We had had our rows previously but had remained on friendly terms.

However this time there was no return to friendly terms. Nothing would evidently convince Simon that I was not a serious contribution to his unpopularity and failure. He embarked upon a series of petty and mean efforts to make me resign, and with each one I became the more determined to stay on and compel him to sack me. I knew that so far as the outside world went I should not be the loser therefrom. And then just before Christmas 1934 he asked me to resign. I told him that dismissal was the only way in which he could get rid of me, that my dismissal was bound to become public property, and that the press, in which I had many friends, would consider that he was malevolently penalizing me for my failure to achieve the impossible at Geneva. I told him what that impossible had been. He asked me to remember that I was speaking to the secretary of state. As I was leaving the room he urged me rather anxiously, I flattered myself, to reconsider my refusal to resign and I said I would think the matter over and let Vansittart have my decision after the Christmas holiday.

I told Vansittart that I would resign, that all the kindness I had received in the past from him and the Office in general outweighed recent bad treatment. I told him what I meant to do. He promised me all the assistance I wanted from himself and the Office. He was as good as his word and so were other ex-colleagues, many of whom felt as he and I did about Germany. The war parted our ways. I only saw him once again. I was driving a large car out of London along Western Avenue during a blitz. After shedding my commuter passengers I stopped at a red light. A small Vauxhall drew up beside me and an angry face poked out and asked where my passengers were. "Same place as your manners I would think." The face stiffened and then grinned. "Arthur, you out of seven millions," it exclaimed.

The months following my departure from official life remain most happily in my memory. I was afforded flattering proof by two large formal lunches given by the British diplomatic and lobby corespondents and by the Foreign Press Association that what I had told Simon at our final interview was right. My old friend, Roderick Jones, the head of Reuters Agency, presided over the English lunch and spoke words more than kind. He read telegrams from the International Association of Correspondents at Geneva and from the British and American Journalists in Paris about "Sir Arthur Willert's unfailing kindness, courtesy and co-operation" and about "his many friends and admirers," and so on. I left the lunch with a lovely silver rose bowl, which has sat ever since on my dining room table.

The lunch of the Foreign Press Association went much the same way. It was presided over by Jean Massip, the representative of the *Petit Parisien,* a level-headed, thoughtful man and a friend of everybody in the News Department. He spoke of the services I had rendered to his association as a go-between with the government. I, on my side, thanked him and his predecessor for all they had done to help me and said that they and many of their colleagues had, especially in the last few years, given the diplomats and politicians an object lesson as to how peace might be consolidated.

I was soon satisfactorily launched in my new career. Paul, who was working his way up in the publishing trade at Heinemann's, introduced me to its head, Charles Evans. I told Evans that I wanted to write a book on behalf of collective security. He agreed, saying: "A reporter's book rather than a student's book." I asked my agent to clinch matters, which he did satisfactorily. He said that the book would sell in America and demanded details about myself for his colleague in New York. "And," he asked, "what about a lecture tour over there next winter? The lectures help the book, and the book helps the lectures. Are you accustomed to public speaking?" I had not done much public speaking, but I told him about the Williamstown lectures. "That's splendid," he exclaimed. "I did not realize that you were in that class."

CHAPTER 20

Europe — 1936

F. AND I LANDED with our motorcar at Ostend on a sunny May afternoon. The beach was crowded: children paddling, their elders sunning themselves, everything peaceful and relaxed. Then suddenly a fighter plane roared low overhead. Nobody noticed it.

This was a foretaste of the two-dimensional world into which we were coming — ordinary people trying with fair success to live their accustomed lives; governments arming, arranging themselves into two potentially hostile groups as before 1914, with Germany in the foreground of the ominous pattern and England once more dithering in the background.

We entered Germany near Aachen and drove to Berlin in leisurely fashion. The country was as agreeable and welcoming as it always had been: the customs officers helpfully civil, the hotels cheap and comfortable. The industrial districts were neat and clean but uncannily silent. The roads were empty until we approached Berlin. Only then did "Heil Hitlers" start and the army and air force spring into evidence, but not offensively; officers and men were young and cheerful and drove considerately. In Berlin friends had taken us rooms in the best hotel. They were extraordinarily cheap and we suspected Nazi propaganda, for the friends were the Dufour Feronces (he had been counselor of the German Embassy in London for years), and they were well in with the party as we discovered the next night when we dined with them.

There were sixteen guests. The serious talk was a preview of what we were to hear from all Nazis high and low. Russia was the danger; Czechoslovakia, so heavily armed, would be her active ally; the aggressive part of *Mein Kampf* was out of date; German rearmament was not for aggression but for defense and to give the people a sense of equality with other nations, to combat unemployment, and, like the labor camps and youth movement, to improve the national stamina. Nobody wanted to grab Austria, an inefficient country that would be a nuisance. Hans Dieckhoff, Dufour's successor in London and now in the Foreign Office, asked me to call on him next day. This I did and had the same record played to me. Dieckhoff was connected by marriage with Ribbentrop, then occupying a vague position in the Foreign Office, of which the oleaginous and arrogant aristocrat, Neurath, was still the head.

A few days later the Ribbentrops invited us to lunch in a pleasant and brightly furnished villa in Dahlem. There were no other guests. Ribbentrop pumped me about England; what influence did Winston Churchill have? As, unfortunately, he had small popular influence then, I said that he had an important following in the Foreign Office. What was thought of Hitler? I said we did not like his treatment of Jews and the churches. Ribbentrop said that we knew nothing of the German Jewish problem. "We have house-broken your Jews before they reach you." His propaganda record was the standard one save that he was extra bitter about Russia. About England he was nauseating. "In Germany's 60,000,000 people there is not one who speaks ill of England."

On one point, however, in the Nazi apologetics non-Nazi Germans and foreigners were in substantial agreement, namely, that Hitler was not coldbloodedly set on war. Ivon Kirkpatrick, afterward head of the Foreign Office and then at our Berlin Embassy, said that Hitler would end up with an army that would go through Europe "like a knife through butter," that he would get the country "magnificently arranged," but that that did not mean that he wanted to fight. His was a policy of bluff and intimidation. The danger was that he might go too far. Why not say this far and no farther? Norman Ebbutt, the very able correspondent of *The Times*, took the same line: Hitler had to be shown the red light, and only England could do it. His colleagues agreed that it was up to us. Ebbutt was not allowed to give full flow to his views in *The Times*. Geoffrey Dawson, as a leading "appeaser," slashed his telegrams about, and remembering what Dawson's support had meant to me in Washington I sympathized deeply with Ebbutt for his lack of it. In the end the Nazis ordered him out, but, owing to Dawson's blue pencil, his offense was primarily what he said about the internal state of Germany.

Two non-Nazis who spoke freely were Peter Reinhold, my lecture colleague at Williamstown, and Rudolf Kirche, editor of the Frankfurter *Zeitung* and formerly its London correspondent. Both were distressed but not in despair; both regretted the political inexperience of the masses who could be deceived, frightened, and regimented to any extent. "The bricks of which the new Germany is being built are patriotism and hope but the mortar is fear," said Reinhold. Both regretted the persecution of the Jews and the churches; both feared war but did not think it inevitable if the other countries stood up to Hitler. Kirche believed that the Reichswehr might be a factor for decency and peace; its officers were no longer the snobs they used to be.

Paul, before joining Heinemann's, had served a publishing apprenticeship with the great Jewish firm of Ullsteins. Its head and his wife took us out to lunch. On our way we passed one of his lorries, and he said, "Where it is going or what it carries, I don't know. I don't even know how long our name will be on it. I have no more control over it than one of our office boys!" At the restaurant some officers of the new air force were gaily feeding. "And I am out of it all," said Ullstein. He had held a captain's commission in the war and now had been ejected from the reserve of officers. His son could never be an officer and he feared they might soon be excluded from citizenship.

We broke our weeks in Berlin by a few days in Danzig where we stayed with the Sean Lesters. He was the commissioner of the League of Nations there. Among such of its inhabitants as we met, there were few illusions about the roughness of Nazism, but they still wanted to go back to Germany. I asked one of them who was a Nazi how this could come about. "Perhaps as part of the peace settlement after the next war," he answered.

For the moment, Danzig seemed to be less interested in its future than in the state of trade. Economic nationalism in Europe was rampant. Tariffs, quotas, manipulated currencies were blocking recovery everywhere. Danzig was worse hit than most places with the mushroom Polish rival of Gdynia a few miles away on the shore of the Polish Corridor. At Danzig a manufacturer said that he had sold a bridge to Bulgaria and had been paid in raisins, nuts, and tobacco, and now he had just heard that one of the Baltic States wanted to give him butter for another bridge. Berlin was buying Brazilian coffee with machinery; Prague was trying to buy cotton from America with beer.

From Berlin we drove to Dresden. Of that delightful town, as it then was, my most vivid memories are of the nightingales in the gardens by the Elbe and of a comfortable German who, while we were listening in the hotel to Hitler on the radio, rose from his seat, uttered loudly a sentence of slang equivalent to "What rot," and walked out. Nobody took it amiss, and next day the "Heil Hitlers" of museum functionaries who were kind to us seemed perfunctory.

From Dresden we entered Czechoslovakia through the pine forests and dull mountains of the Sudetenland, populated mainly by the Germans whose discontents Hitler exploited so ruthlessly. In the afternoon we reached the industrial suburbs of Prague. They might have belonged to any big manufacturing town of America. They were full of movement and lacked the strange apathetic silence of the Rhineland. The streets further in were as crowded and carefree as those of London.

Jan Masaryk called and took us out to dinner. He was then minister in London. He was not, like his father, an outstanding leader. But he had courage, intelligence, honesty, and charm, and his ambition was patriotic and not personal. I never knew him intimately, but I knew him well enough to be certain that when after the 1939 war he returned to his country to help in its reconstruction, he was murdered by the Communists and did not commit suicide as they averred. Masaryk took us to a popular restaurant renowned for its beer. It was full of small businessmen and their womenfolk. They appeared a self-satisfied and cheerful crowd. "You are seeing," Masaryk said, "for the first time since you crossed the Rhine a roomful of free people. We are the only democracy in this part of the world. We can say what we like, write what we like. And we keep our elections free even when under a considerable temptation not to do so."

He displayed the other side of the shield a few days later at lunch at the American legation.

Democracy has paid us so far. But we depend for our existence upon factors outside our control. If Russia and Germany come to blows where should we be? And if Germany acquired Austria without war, we should be right inside the jaws of a great Teutonic State. What would our German minority do then? No: you people in America and England have little idea of the strain under which we and other countries in Central Europe live . . .

Masaryk took us to the President's country residence (the President was ill and we did not see him) for tea and dinner. We met there several Czech notabilities. As everywhere else in Czechoslovakia, one was haunted by an uncanny contradictory feeling of precarious prosperity and lurking danger.

Vienna presented a painful contrast. Austria was torn by conflicting groups, conservative, socialist, communist, Nazi and anti-Nazi, pro-German and pro-Italian. In Vienna alone of all the towns we were in that summer, utter indigence and selfish opulence elbowed each other.

One saw respectable middle-aged couples hopelessly sitting about on the public benches nibbling inadequate sandwiches. "Walked about and saw palaces and poverty," wrote F. We only stayed in Vienna a few days. I saw the obvious people, such as the head of the Foreign Office, the editor of the leading newspaper — both of whom I knew already, *The Times* correspondent and one or two other foreign journalists, and, above all, the American minister, George Messersmith, who, his embassy in Berlin told me, knew more about Central Europe than most people. He was consul general in Berlin when Hitler came into power and he looked upon the Nazis with informed disgust and apprehension:

He said that Hitler would seize Austria at the first opportunity and then Czechoslovakia and probably Poland. Only if Britain and France stood firmly together with Russia could this disaster be avoided. Nothing but a display of organised force would restrain Hitler. Waving bits of paper at him had the same effect as waving cloaks at bulls. Admonitory notes and resolutions simply gave Goebbels ammunition for internal use.

It was a relief to set out for Italy one morning over the sunny

Semmering Pass into the valley of the Drava to the sound of whose rushing waters we slept that night at Villach; next night we were in Venice. We went to Venice hoping to forget the troubles of Europe for a day or two. But at our hotel on the waterfront beyond the ducal palace we were at once confronted by a part of the French fleet (France was courting Italy at that moment). And next morning there was no peace in the Square of St. Mark, which was being prepared for some Fascist celebration. Flags clashed gaudily with the mellow beauty of the church, and a few hours later dark lines of uniforms made energetic patterns in the center of the square. Watching them we found ourselves jammed up against a talkative American. His business had just taken him around most of Europe. He inveighed against what we were watching. He was horrified by all the beating up of militant nationalism, which contradicted so tragically the universal desire of individuals for peace. We agreed, and nowhere was this discrepancy more noticeable than in Italy. Our glimpse of the country was fleeting — the ordinary travelers' conversations and a few days in Milan, where we had friends.

"Better than I shall be getting in 'Abyssinia' by Christmas" was the answer of a waiter to a compliment upon the food he was serving us. There were fears that Mussolini was sacrificing Italy's position in Europe to a doubtful gamble in Africa. He would, I noted, need a spectacular success in Abyssinia not to be in trouble at home. I also noted the failure of the newspaper campaign he was conducting against us for being less tolerant of his African adventure than the French. Everybody was as friendly as possible.

From Milan we drove to Genoa and then over the fine road the Fascists had built along the coast into France and on to Cap d'Antibes. There I wrote for six hours a day and bathed in the sea and sun for about three weeks. The book fell easily into shape. I quickly regained something of my journalistic knack of writing speedily, if roughly. I was sure of my thesis. Hitler was bluffing his way to international power. He did not want war; nobody wanted war. But unless shown the red light he would go from outrage to outrage until his bluff simply had to be called. That would mean war. Piecemeal rearmament of the democracies would not show the red light. We British must take the lead with the French. At the same time we must not penalize Germany on account of Hitler, economically or otherwise, as that would only play into his hands. The more comfortable the German population the less appeal Goebbels' propaganda would have.

We spent some time in Geneva and Paris on the way back. In Paris views were various. In Geneva my thesis of collective security and no talk about "keeping Germany lean" tallied with the general opinion. The stock of British statesmanship stood lower than ever.

Back in England I settled down at home to three months of writing, broken by occasional days in London. They were good months. The summer was fine and the garden at its best. I called the book *The Frontiers of England* and gave it to Heinemann's in October and it was out well before Christmas. I was surprised and encouraged by its reception. Best of all I liked this note from Lord Cecil of Chelwood:

> I have just finished reading your admirable book on the 'Frontiers of England' and am impelled to write and thank you for having written it . . . As you can imagine, I heartily agree with the recommendations you make and I trust it will have a very wide sale.

Philip Gibbs, who had written a rather similar book the year before, Freddie Voight, Norman Ewer, and others whose judgment I valued were extremely flattering. *The Times*, in spite of its appeasement propensities, said that I was fair-minded and stated my conclusions with "great lucidity and cogency." But best of all reviews I liked Robert Lind, who compared the book to a first-rate wireless talk with the flavor of personal experience. And that was precisely the sort of book that I had tried to write.

Later on when it appeared in America, Frank Simonds welcomed me back from officialdom to my real trade by saying that when he saw me functioning as a press officer at conferences, he used to think of Clemenceau's remark when Paderewski deserted the piano for the presidency of Poland: "What a comedown."

CHAPTER 21

The American Lecture Circuit

I MADE THREE TEN-WEEK LECTURE TOURS in the United States that started in January in 1936, 1937, and 1939. I embarked nervously on the first one. I had never once spoken in public while living in Washington.

F. crossed the Atlantic with me to pay visits in various parts of the country. Her first visit was to the White House when I accompanied her for a night and was somewhat reassured by President Roosevelt. "You will be all right," he said. "You have a good voice; you know what you want to say. All you have to do is to be conversational; don't lecture; hold your head up and speak up."

I did not see much of the President. There was a big dinner party on our first evening, and on the second the President went to the capitol to deliver his annual message. We dined with him and some of his family and it did not make me any happier to notice that even he was stealing glances at his speech on his knee under the table throughout the meal. We went to the capitol with Eleanor Roosevelt, and I was back in familiar surroundings, though not now in the press gallery but opposite it.

The floor of the House of Representatives filled gradually,

the senators entered in procession, the Cabinet took its place in front of the rostrum. The President appeared, supported by his eldest son, James. The address was interrupted by Democratic cheers and once by ironic Republican laughter. We returned to the White House; the President joined us and called, I think, for Ovaltine. His family teased him about his speech and he responded in kind. Telegrams, mainly congratulatory, began to pour in. He particularly liked praise from people who were not chronic admirers. The party broke up well after midnight and James Roosevelt and I caught a train to New York. I was told that there would be a bed for me at the White House whenever I proposed myself.

At the large lunch of the Foreign Policy Association, a formidable first audience, nervousness left me the moment I rose and they seemed satisfied. F. rang up to say that on the radio I had sounded quite the practiced speaker. The next stop on my tour was at Lexington, Massachusetts. My diary does not mention the lecture so I suppose it went all right. It records that my host took me to its common where the first blood of the American Revolution was shed and told me that when a few years ago he had done the same for a leading member of the British Bar, a guest of the American Bar Association in Boston, and had said to him: "Here is where the battle was fought," the Englishman said, "What, one of your scraps with the Indians?" "British humor, perhaps?" my host asked me. "No," I said, "typical British ignorance of things American." My host refused to identify the Englishman but said that he was not unknown in politics.

After Lexington came the Harvard Club in Boston, notoriously one of the most critical audiences in the country. Everything went well. Felix Frankfurter, not long back at Harvard from his spell as Eastman professor at Oxford, introduced me with a flattering charm that did much to bring me together with the rows of faces in front of me, and next day, the secretary of the club wrote to my agent:

> It has seldom been my privilege to write so earnestly and enthusiastically as I can about Sir Arthur Willert. He chose to talk in a conversational manner with our members and he chose wisely because he established a feeling of confidence between that very large group of men and himself. Everybody was delighted with the way in which he handled his question and answer period and particularly at the ease with which he did it.

This was relayed to me a little later by my agent and with it came the verdict of a women's club near Pittsburgh:

> I am very happy to say that I heard many enthusiastic remarks upon Sir Arthur Willert and upon his talk which was very gratifying to the Board. We certainly hope to have him with us again. He is an able speaker from beginning to end.

Pats on the back from such dissimilar hands gave me the self-confidence I needed. I found that I liked lecturing. I liked trying to tailor my subject to suit different audiences in different parts of the country. I usually had to speak on Europe. There was anxious desire to know what was going on there.

There followed a hectic zigzagging up, down, and across the Eastern portion of the United States. Chicago and Topeka were as far west as I penetrated, Miami and St. Paul, north and south. I met old friends and acquaintances and made new ones. I learned a lot about current American thought. I was entertained at lunches and dinners, from the meager salad and ice cream meals of women's clubs to the solidity of Rotary luncheons, and the white tie dinners of the English-Speaking Unions. I enjoyed most and gained most from my university and college audiences — I spent hours in the smoking compartments of trains listening to commercial travelers discussing the state of business or of their insides and the amenities, or the reverse, of the towns they visited. I was lucky in the three breaks in my program, as they landed me in Chicago, St. Louis, and Washington, places in which I could relax pleasantly with friends.

From Chicago I was hustled off to St. Paul to speak to the local branch of the Foreign Policy Association. I arrived there early in the morning in intense cold, so cold that the inside of the inside pane of the double window of the Pullman was frosted over. But the air was so dry that it did not feel uncomfortable, and in the evening I walked to where I was to eat and lecture in thin dress shoes.

On my way southward I spent a night and gave a lecture at Janesville in Wisconsin. It was my first experience of a smallish Middle Western community and a delightful one. Kind strangers put me up and gave me a party. Though Janesville had its industries (it was, and probably still is, the home of the Parker Pen), there was none of Sinclair Lewis's Babbittry about what I saw of it.

On the pretext of wanting to think over my lecture I took a walk through streets and avenues, most of them lined with trees, bordered by detached houses with their lawns and general air of neatness and quiet self-respecting civilization. My hosts lived in one of them. They were liberals; they approved with some reservations of the New Deal. They took in the weekly edition of the Manchester *Guardian* and in the summer usually crossed the Atlantic. They were units of a cultivated close-knit local governing society, and they seemed to be on good democratic terms with those below them.

From Janesville I returned to Chicago, gave another lecture, and proceeded to St. Louis. There the old friends were Lionberger Davis and his wife; he was a banker and a leading citizen. They had a large house in a quiet inner suburb, in the dining room of which I met my first electric toaster. The few other friends I had in the town were asked to see me. My host was delighting in a new car and showed me the sights of the

neighborhood of which I recall the confluence of the Missouri
and the Mississippi, the one clear gray, the other muddy brown.
They flowed side by side in the same channel for some way
without mingling.

I have a grateful memory of the first of several visits to
Topeka, where I addressed Washburn College, and I was
touched to discover in my hotel room a bottle of whiskey, Prohibition having lingered on in Kansas. Another good memory
of those first weeks is of Lexington, Kentucky. I had never in
all my years in Washington been further south than Richmond
and Norfolk because the South was still so far outside the main
flow of events. I was surprised by the Southern atmosphere of
Lexington: separate waiting rooms for whites and blacks at the
station, an untidy main street, buildings Victorian. Private
houses built of brick sometimes painted white with large windows and green shutters, fine trees for summer shade in the
streets and squares. The house I stayed in was more than
a century old and unchanged save for electric lights and other
modern essentials. The furniture was of plain, heavy mahogany, and some of the chairs and sofas were covered with horse-
hair cloth. The lofty rooms were separated from each other by
large white doors that could be left open in summer for air.
There were family portraits on the walls. I was greeted by a
tea of delicate ham sandwiches, scones, cake served around by
a dignified colored butler in a white jacket.

I was soon to have a much bigger dose of the South. After a
rush around in the snows of Ontario and New England I found
myself in New York taking the train for Florida. I reveled
in that journey. I had long ago learned to appreciate the comfort of long-distance traveling in America in those days — the
steady trains, the excellent service and food — especially break-
fasts, the well-cleaned windows. And I used the windows on
that trip.

I went to bed as we left Washington and woke up somewhere in North Carolina. I performed the well-practiced contortions of dressing on my becurtained shelf with the bottom of the upper berth about three feet above it, hurried to the restaurant, and ordered my breakfast and looked out eagerly. And that morning and for the rest of the day I thought I understood why the South was outside the stream of American life. A traveler in the North passed much untidiness in the train between New York and Philadelphia, for example, on the waterfront of St. Louis as viewed from the railway bridge over the Mississippi, on the outskirts, indeed, of most towns big and small, but it was the untidiness of progress, whereas my first impression of the South was that its untidiness sprang from stagnation. Here are some notes I scribbled on the train that day and the next:

Untidy brown country. Cotton fields still unploughed; stalks of plants occasionally decorated with white tassels of cotton; sometimes a whole field so decorated, too poor to be picked. Maize the only other crop. Red soil. The occasional high roads seemed to have no connection with the country, nor did the glossy cars upon them or parked in the unkempt station squares.

Pine trees, oaks ragged with dry leaves, glossy magnolias standing out among all the raggedness like a tall hat among caps. It was something though to see the earth again and unfrozen puddles after weeks of snow: nice to see people without coats, the gay dresses and splashes of colour of children going to school. But the incredible squalor of it all! the unpainted hovels and dilapidated houses, the dirt roads. The houses placed haphazard on the land, without gardens with only a greater untidiness around them, a number of them uninhabited ruins, some with only brick fireplaces and chimney left, the gaunt tombstones of dead hearths.

Florida better. Not much settled in the days of slavery. Great green stretches of open country, acres of French beans sometimes being picked by bands of negroes. Dead flat; shaggy patches of palmetto. Cattle herded by a mounted cowboy alongside an aerodrome. Buzzards slowly wheeling, like bloated flies, over rubbish dumps, clear ponds with water lilies and other flowers.

At Miami one was back in the North, but for the soft sea air, the hot sun, the palm trees, and tropical flowers. I breakfasted and lunched at the hotel that the taxi driver who picked me up at the station recommended. It was good and expensive. I hired a car for the morning and drove about; the tall buildings of Miami seen from Miami Beach resembled a fragment of New York dumped on a sandy island in a tropical lagoon. It contained, even then I was told, about 120,000 inhabitants all living on its visitors whose motorcars were parked everywhere and came from every state in the Union, though principally Ohio, New York, and New Jersey. We drove along great boulevards, half luxury, half desert. A house, a neat garden, a group of drunken-looking coconut palms, a vacant lot with palmetto scrub, and dumps of empty tins and rubbish — and so on.

I took a train for Palm Beach that afternoon. My host met me and settled me into a comfortable club. The club was in the center of the little town, the architecture of which I told myself was "Italo-Iberian." Luxury shops lined the streets. It was rather like Cannes in the old days. I was taken to my hosts' house to a large and agreeable dinner party, and I rather think I gave my lecture there. Anyhow my audience was small, select, and savagely conservative. To it the President was anti-Christ; the Communists were inciting the Negroes to revolt. Next day a morning in the sun sightseeing, drinks at a country club with a swimming pool, a glimpse of a blue sea with the gulf stream (I seem to remember) running brown a few miles out.

From Palm Beach I went to Atlanta. I had enjoyed my glimpse of Palm Beach and had appreciated the trouble taken to entertain me, but I was glad to have a couple of early spring days with the forsythia and daffodils in bloom in a spacious modern city on the slopes of the inland uplands. The people

I met, the two audiences I talked to, revealed a new South that did not stagnate. So did a stay at Athens, Georgia, where I delivered a couple of lectures for the University of Georgia and where modern thinking and planning and the old Southern ways of domestic life seemed to me to have made an admirable marriage. From Athens another long jump to Baltimore where I addressed the local Foreign Policy Association and Culture Club, and then Washington and the White House before final flings at Philadelphia, Providence, and Boston. I had given over fifty lectures in ten weeks to every conceivable sort of audience, from girls' schools upward, and I had added to my bank account in Toronto some particularly valuable dollars, for money in those days earned, banked, and spent abroad was immune from taxation at home. Thus lecturing in America more than paid for expensive holidays and tours in Europe.

My 1937 tour was over much the same territory as in 1936 save that I did not go south. Instead I spent more time in New England, very beautiful under its coat of snow, though by the end of March when I gave my last lecture at Montpelier, the capital of Vermont, spring was in the air and the sap rising in the sugar maples with tins attached to the trunks to catch it as it flowed from the cuts in the bark. In the lower valleys the snow was melting fast in the warmth of the sun, sliding off the roofs of the old wooden bridges over the streams. In the villages and small towns the branches of the weeping elms that beautify the streets were taking on the red-brown bloom of early spring.

It had been a thoroughly satisfactory tour. No missed train connections (my agent would not allow his clients to fly, at least not in winter, lest they should be delayed by fog, storm, or mechanical defect), no unexpectedly canceled meetings, no untoward incidents, no long unbroken series of nights in sleeping cars.

My next and last tour was in 1939. My agent had been begging me to come again and I agreed to, provided that he sent me out to the Pacific Coast. At Charleston, West Virginia, the ordeal started!

I arrived there on a rainy morning after a night journey, and before leaving that night wrote:

> Why did I ever take to lecturing? I ring up the person who I had been informed was responsible for my lecture; his telephone was disconnected. I go through the rain to the hall I was supposed to lecture in. A good-natured caretaker says that it was not booked that evening. I ring up New York. They were profusely sorry. The talk had been cancelled some time since and they had somehow or other not told me. I reverse the charge for the call: the only possible revenge.
>
> Lecturers are defenceless creatures. They are catapulted hither or thither. Their's not reason why: their's only to catch inconvenient trains, to sleep, wash and eat as best they can and to deliver the goods to their audiences. They are speeded up as no worker in a Detroit automobile factory is. The difference is that their tours don't go on indefinitely. Three months would be about all human endurance could stand . . .
>
> The rain plunges down; across the road the puddles encroach upon the greasy earth of a disconsolate motor park in a vacant lot where the bright paintwork of several new cars look as incongruous as a ball-dress in a coal cellar. Motors in this country often do strike a note of incongruity. The other day I was travelling in a day coach across the mining country near here, the country of Conan Doyle's 'Valley of Fear'. We stopped at a way-side station; a miner with the grime of the pit still on his face climbed into the train from a shining Buick and bundled into it a slattern wife who had been sitting across from me.

On February 10 I wrote while on the train in southern Texas:

> How I am travelling! Today is Friday. I left New York a fortnight ago and since then have only had five nights in a bed. And by the time I reach San Francisco a week tomorrow my score will have been 14 nights out of 18 on the train.

From Charleston I had gone by night to Wheeling where I

arrived about six, breakfasted, and took a room for a couple of hours to shave and bathe in a dilapidated and dismal hotel. Outside wet snow was falling and the Ohio River swirled by in a hissing brown flood. I caught a train to Morgantown to speak at West Virginia University. Soon the snow turned to rain and the West Virginia "black industrial country" was revealed to me in all its jaundiced beastliness. The rain soaked down upon the squalor from low, tawny clouds through a yellow mist and poured off the brown and rocky hills into swollen streams, so loaded with yellow mud that they looked oily and solid; one was seeing an aspect of the soil erosion problem that Franklin Roosevelt was trying to tackle. The talk of the passengers who got on and off the day coach at each stop was all about the floods. The river was full of driftwood and other flotsam. A woman remarked upon it. "Did you see those two dead men way back?" asked her husband. There was a chorus of feminine consternation. "Nor did I," said he.

At Morgantown I was caught up in its pleasant academic hospitality and forgot about the elements for a while. But when we went from dinner to the lecture hall the rain had turned to snow and by the time we came out everything was covered. This was bad, as one of the faculty was going to drive me to Connellsville about forty miles away, where I had to catch a train to Cleveland. I persuaded him to allow me to take a taxi whose driver was said to be very reliable. And so he proved. The roads were slippery, but the snow stopped and the moon came out, and I enjoyed the keen air and the easy conversation of my companion. At the station I had to wait about three hours for the train in a waiting room so overheated that from time to time I went outside to breathe. Nor was I allowed to doze; there were a couple of train hands about with nothing to do who were inquisitive about the prospects of another European war and so on. I reached Cleveland at eight-thirty, breakfasted, spoke to the City Club at lunch, and took the train that night for St. Louis, with the comforting prospect of a quiet Sunday with my friends there.

Two talks on Monday: the English-Speaking Union for the third time. Night train to Chicago; day's journey to Ames, Iowa; hurried change; dinner, lecture for University of Iowa; social half-hour; slippery drive to station as snowing again; night train to Topeka; out into a world glazed by frozen rain; another talk at Washburn College but talk curtailed as was due at Rotary Club for lunch and President Woomer's car had skidded into impotent inextricability on the way from the station and no taxi available; after lunch, local train to junction to catch night train to Dallas.

Thence day train to San Marcos in southwest Texas. Here the outlook is more cheerful. The misty, flat landscape is flooded with sunlight. For the first time since I landed I see green grass, people at the stations are without great coats, groups of workmen take their midday rest basking in the sun. There are masses of mistletoe in the trees; magnolias and cypress, wallflowers and daffodils in the gardens. The tortured valleys of West Virginia and icy streets of Topeka belong to another world. Later in another train I write gratefully of San Marcos. I bathe and sleep in a bed there. I give a talk in their "Celebrity Series"; I am taken next day into the country, which I find rather like the hills of southern France. Then the night train to Forth Worth, hurried change next morning; into train for Denver where I arrive next morning; hurried change into another train, which takes me through the Rocky Mountains in a day and a night to Provo, near Salt Lake City, a beautifully situated town where I talk at Brigham Young University and sleep in a bed; next day short journey to Salt Lake City; night train to Pendleton, Oregon, where I hang about for a few hours and then take a bus to Colfax, Washington, where I change into another bus and arrive very late at Pullman, Washington, where I speak at the state college next morning. Then short bus drive to Spokane and address local English-Speaking Union in evening. Another night in bed; a lovely day journey down the Columbia River to Portland, Oregon. Leave Portland that evening for San Francisco, where I arrive late next day after a beautiful journey through northern California.

At San Francisco the pace slackened. I spent four days there with only two lectures and a third at nearby Sacramento. Then a couple of quiet days at Santa Barbara with friends and only one lecture; an entertaining glimpse of Hollywood society and across the desert to Albuquerque, in New Mexico, and again only one lecture and two or three days with Ruth McCormick and her new husband, Albert Simms, on her ranch (Medill had died prematurely in 1925). Then more intensive strenuosity: Amarillo and Lubbock in the Panhandle of Texas in a dust storm, Houston, Galveston, Dallas, Tulsa, Chicago, some other Middle Western dates, Toronto and London, Ontario, Olean in New York State, a weekend in Washington, a cluster of dates in New England, and the *Normandie* to Southampton.

So ended my venture on the American lecture circuit. I should not have continued it even if war had not intervened. I was fifty-seven and would soon be too old for the ruthless exploitation that one was expected to endure a generation and more ago.

CHAPTER 22

The Rooseveltian Neutrality — 1939

THE STRENUOSITIES of my lecture tours were more than re-
paid by the opportunities they afforded to appraise the
attitude of America toward the gathering crisis. I needed to
know American opinion for writing and lecturing purposes
when I got home. Opportunities to learn ranged all the way
from the casual contacts of Pullman smoking compartments or
hotel bars to visits to local newspaper offices, question periods
at lectures, informal meetings with teachers and students at
colleges or schools, and a comparison of views with old friends
from the President downward. Everywhere there was an under-
tone of anxiety, sometimes informed, sometimes instinctive.
It was quite different from 1914. Then the war had come as
a spectacle, tragic but remote without direct interest to the
United States as a country until war trade began to make it so.

Now the interest was direct, owing to the cruel, brutal ambitions of Hitler and his gang, and to the stories about their extent, which, since the disintegration of the Geneva Disarmament
Conference, were being sent home by the extremely competent
corps of American newspaper correspondents and radio reporters in Europe. Everywhere one discovered appreciation of what
the Nazi menace could mean to the world.

I never, not even in 1939, returned to England without being ashamed of the contrast between American apperception and British apathy. I was speaking and writing a lot at home in support of collective security. I was reporting ad nauseam the apprehensions of Germany's neighbors and of the international experts at Geneva. I spoke to highly sophisticated audiences and more often to popular ones. One was listened to and questioned with apparent interest. I hope my articles were read in the same way. But neither what I nor what many better qualified and more important people had to say had much effect. The League of Nations Union worked hard over its Peace Ballot. The Ballot showed 11,000,000 votes for sanctions against law-breaking aggressors and 8,000,000 for restraint by arms if sanctions failed.

Why could not this nucleus of practical sense be developed into national policy? The answer, I felt at the time, was that the British, chronically indifferent to the outside world, were absorbed in their own affairs. They were recovering rather better from the great slump of the early thirties than their competitive countries. Only rousing leadership from a trusted source could make them raise their eyes. And that was not forthcoming. The government and a powerful section of the press were in the clutches of the appeasers, people who regarded Bolshevist Russia a more instant danger than Hitler's Germany. Some indeed envisaged Hitler as a possible bolster between us and the Kremlin. The only rousing politician who saw things straight was Winston Churchill. He did his best to drive home the German danger. He failed for reasons outside the ambit of this book and was regarded in America as a failed politician. His name was not often mentioned. I have no record, nor memory, for instance, of its coming up in the various conversations I had with the President.

What the Americans wanted was a Britain that would, with France, take the lead in ringing Germany around by countries so strongly armed and combined that Hitler would think twice before continuing his program of acquisition by bluff. Few of them envisaged the possibility of their supporting such an organization actively. The demand of Congress for insulated neutrality had the backing of a very definite majority. I used to feel that we British were looked upon very much as the police force is looked upon by the inhabitants of the peaceful part of a gangster-ridden community: it must be strong enough to keep their quarter safe from the gangsters.

It cannot be said that there was much confidence that we could carry out that role. In all my three tours I found our politicians and their policies under heavy fire. In 1936 the Hoare-Laval Agreement gave me much trouble. Americans thought it sold Abyssinia down the river to Mussolini. Here Baldwin was unfairly blamed. "That man, 'Baldwin,' he sure did make a poor showing over that Hoare-Laval Agreement," remarked a barber out of the blue at Baltimore as I sat in his chair. Sophisticated observers asked inconvenient questions as to the identity of Hoare's professional advisers who had allowed him to make the blunder. One sheltered oneself behind the promptitude with which public and parliamentary indignation forced Baldwin to scrap the agreement and sack Hoare.

The next year Baldwin was blamed for having forced Edward VIII off the throne. He was regarded as a cynical conservative who maneuvered the King into exile because the King was too radical and (somewhat illogically) because he frequented circles that Ribbentrop (then Nazi ambassador in London) also frequented. Here I found that the best course was to fall back upon the impregnable solidity of the British monarchy.

Our war debt was another prickly subject, especially in 1937, when Neville Chamberlain, then Chancellor of the Exchequer, revealed himself to be as arrogantly ignorant of America as he was of Europe. "British arguments against paying," he was re-

ported to have said in public, "may not appeal to the Middle
West, but I think will appeal to the more responsible sections
of opinion in the United States." Walter Runciman, President
of the Board of Trade, on his way to Washington to discuss
the American proposal for a freer trading treaty with us and
others, when asked by a reporter whether he would also be
discussing war debts, snapped: "God forbid."

In 1939, Munich and our failure to save Austria were, of
course, the red rags. Chamberlain and his umbrella were objects of contemptuous ridicule: "Do you know what the Czechs
call him? *J'aime Berlin.*" It was suggested that there was a
secret understanding between him and Hitler that Germany
could do what she liked in Central and Eastern Europe if she
sided with Britain and France against Russia. I welcomed this
calumny. I was not prepared to defend Munich as my friend
Ronald Storrs was doing or to proclaim that war was now quite
inevitable as my friend André Géraud (Pertinax) was doing.
So I was grateful for one attack on Chamberlain that could be
emphatically refuted. Eden, whose descent upon New York
after he had left office had not helped us or himself, gave me
another good talking point. He was reported to have said that
we could get along without American money and supplies in
the case of war. I was constantly asked whether this was the
British view. I replied, indeed I volunteered, that it was not,
that we should welcome all the American help we could get.
This, I noted, "went like hot cakes."

One did not, however, have to travel far before one realized
that, if the stock of British politicians was low, that of Britain
as a country was higher than it had been in 1914. Not only were
the anti-British German and Irish "hyphenates" weaker, the
Indian nationalists seemed to have faded out and dislike of
British colonialism seemed to be more marked in Washington than in the country.

All this strengthened an influence that I had always regarded as a constant in the Anglo-American relationship, namely, that beneath the surface eddies of distrust, irritation, and criticism there runs a constant current of good will flowing from a common language (the theory that this is a cause of misunderstanding has always seemed paradoxical nonsense to me) and from the British way of life being more like the American way than those of other countries. Sometimes that current comes to the surface.

The death of George V was a case in point. I crossed the border from Canada a few days after it, and American mourning was nearly as marked as Canadian. Congress suspended a session, the press was full of eulogy and sympathy, strangers condoled with one, and there were memorial services. Even in Chicago, a great Anglophobic center, crowds attended a service. I stayed there shortly afterward with Frank McCoy, the general commanding the Chicago district, and he told me that he and his staff had gone to it in uniform and that, rather to his surprise, there were no protests against this Anglophile gesture of the American army.

One was occasionally treated to unexpected bursts of this latent pro-British feeling. I wrote, for instance, in a tram in North Carolina:

> The conductor, a cadaverous, drawling Southerner, took me for a Texan. I said, "English." His face lighted up. "I like the English. I listen to them on the radio every day! A fine service . . . We are the only two civilized countries." I asked whether he listened to the Germans. He said, "No, I hate those people. That guy Hitler is a public menace."

One met this fear and loathing of Hitler at every turn, even among those of German origin. Out in Utah, a rough sheep farmer had told me that he did not see how the world could settle down until Hitler had been "bumped off." "Why," I asked, "do you feel so strongly?" "I have heard him on the air." At Lubbock in Texas a seller of newspapers exclaimed in great excitement that the radio had just announced that Hitler had been assassinated. I said that this was indeed great news. "Yes," he replied, "it sure is, and I hope they get that man Goering, too. May as well give that lot the whole works." At Portland, Oregon, I saw a film that started about the power of the printed word. The Bible was shown as still being the best seller. But the Bible was being hard pressed by other books, by Lenin's works (silence), by *Mein Kampf* (hisses). After the American Constitution (cheers) came the American Boy Scout movement and its excellence in democracy, then British and French Boy Scouts (cheers), then German jackboots (hisses). It was a clever film with its implications of democratic solidarity.

But the greatest reassurance as to the fundamental position of the United States, if the worst came, was to be found in the White House. The atmosphere there was so utterly different from that which permeated it during the Wilsonian neutrality. Toward the end of my 1939 tour, knowing that Eleanor Roosevelt was away, I wrote to Miss LeHand, the President's secretary, to ask whether I could spend a weekend at the White House. She telegraphed back, "President very sorry. Expects to be in Georgia March 26th but hopes you will stop at the White House while you are in Washington." I was flattered and disappointed, and descended on other friends.

On my arrival I discovered that the President had not gone south after all, telephoned the White House, and was invited to dinner that night. It was a congenial evening. Franklin Roosevelt had characteristically taken the trouble to collect some of my old friends, Felix Frankfurter and Francis Biddle among them. Politics were not touched upon but the President asked me to come in next afternoon for a long talk.

Next afternoon I was put onto the sofa near the fireplace in the upstairs study and was kept there till nearly dinner time. The President thought that the odds upon a European war in

1939 were about fifty-fifty. His indignation at Chamberlain's refusal to let him have a hand in trying to settle the trouble the year before still smoldered. He spoke about his readiness to make another effort. But his immediate concern was the education of his countrymen to allow him to take all the steps short of fighting to help the Allies if war came.

He radiated consciousness of power and self-confidence. Self-confidence, saved from the taint of conceit by charm and salted by flippancy, always seemed to me to be his chief characteristic. On an earlier visit to the White House, he had discoursed upon the difficulties of the New Deal. Among them he mentioned the size of the country. I asked him what he thought of the idea then being mooted of assistant regional Presidents. He said the solution would not be a safe one. He himself would risk it. But the time might come when one of the assistants was strong and the President weak; then there might be insubordination, to the point of revolt.

He cared nothing for the virulent hostility to the New Deal by those who earned or owned much money. When I was lecturing at Palm Beach, a little old man with a neat beard in the first row of my opulent audience asked me whether I had heard that the New Deal had been invented by a Jewish professor in London. I told this to the President. "Harold Laski," he exclaimed and laughed. Then very seriously: "The fools! Cannot they see that I am protecting them from the deluge?"

The President was bitter about appeasement. He had no use for Chamberlain. He thought Simon and Samuel Hoare about the worst foreign ministers we had ever had — Simon as shown up by the disarmament conference, Hoare by the Hoare-Laval Agreement. It was not the first time that I had heard Rooseveltian impatience at British lack of statesmanship. I happened to be at the White House when Hitler marched into the demilitarized zone of the Rhineland in 1936. Roosevelt inquired what I thought we and the French would do. I said we should write notes but nothing more. "Won't that simply mean postponing war for a few years by when Hitler will be much better prepared, and you not so much better?" was the sense of his reply. Next day, when it was clear that Hitler had got away with it, he said that he could understand our unwillingness to get tough with the Japanese over Manchuria. The American people wouldn't fight for China any more than the British. But Abyssinia and now the Rhineland, and soon probably Austria: why did we not prepare a European front that would show the dictators that force could not pay?

That was in 1936. Now in 1939 the President said that he had just heard from a source that had so far served him well that encouraged by our spinelessness, Hitler was planning aggression in Eastern Europe for 1939, against France in 1940, then against Britain, and finally, helped by Japan, against the United States.

The President said that the two chief obstacles in the way of preparing the United States morally and materially to help the democracies were: first, Congress and its neutrality legislation and second, the fact that four out of five Americans were instinctively against the League of Nations and Old World entanglements. But he thought he was having some success with Congress. I would have noticed the sensation aroused by a story that he had told some senators that the American frontier was on the Rhine. What he had really said was that the American defenses started in Finland and went on through the Scandinavian countries to the other democracies. He had told the senators that last August he would have named Czechoslovakia as part of these defenses. But it had now gone, and the weaker the democracies grew in Europe the worse for the United States. That was the sort of argument he was using in private conversation. He was also playing up aerial vulnerability. Spain, North Africa, the Azores, northeast Brazil, and Yucatán were stages to places like Houston.

Roosevelt had just been out with the fleet on maneuvers and had been prophetically impressed by the profound change that the airplane would bring to naval warfare. He said that he was giving much thought to ways in which the American navy could help us. He would have to declare certain waters like the eastern Atlantic and the Mediterranean areas of belligerency out of which American shipping must keep, and he did not see why the American navy should not patrol the waters outside those areas. Then the British navy could concentrate where most needed. Having expatiated upon the efficiency of the American fleet, he exclaimed, "If yours is as good, and if we stand together we will show the dictators that democracy can still look after itself."

We turned to Spain. The President did not think that we British had looked after ourselves there. He thought that Franco would be forced to join the dictators if war came. I said that our trouble regarding Spain was obsolescent conservatism. He agreed. If I would forgive him for saying so, the weakness of our present government was too much Eton and Oxford. The Spanish aristocracy were pleasant people. The Spanish Queen was English. The other side were bourgeois or lower. They were mixed up with Russia and local communism to some extent, and that was enough to make British conservatives take the wrong side and fail to see the real issue in the Civil War.

The President reminded me that two years ago he had told me that he thought it was most important that Franco should not be allowed to be the thin end of the dictatorial wedge in Spain. How difficult it was to make one's views known confidentially. He had never hidden his feelings about Spain in private conversation, yet Neville Chamberlain had thought him pro-Franco.

He was disappointed with Mussolini whom, like many in England, he had regarded in spite of Abyssinia as a leader with whom cooperation might be possible. He had just been listening to him on the radio. He had informed the Italian ambassador the week before, in reply to certain indirect unofficial hints from Mussolini, that he was prepared to initiate another move for a conference on something of the sort if Mussolini really thought it would do good. He had hoped for some sort of response in the Duce's wireless talk. There had been none. He thought that success in Spain had strengthened the Duce with his people and that propaganda for the annexation of Nice, Savoy, Tunis, etc., etc., had influenced them. He had told the Italian ambassador that if war came, he would do all he could to help the democracies. I thought that this rebuff had gone far to convince him that Mussolini would stand with Hitler.

He hoped to goodness that we should go in for conscription. The United States would do so at once if they got into war, but not before. I said that an obstacle to our so acting now was the Labour Party — the question of conscription of wealth, etc. I asked what he would do about all that. He said he would give the millionaire executive (if he could make the rank) the pay of a major-general and that the worker should be given approximately the same as he had been making in peacetime. "Very expensive," I said. "No," he replied, "not really. Most of the money would go back into circulation and come back to the government in taxes, etc." After more vague talk of this kind the President exclaimed that whatever might be worked out he was confident that "our demo-plutocracies would not go down in financial ruin."

The above is a slightly abridged transcript of the notes I made the same evening of my last conversation with Franklin Roosevelt. I found it a most encouraging conversation. As the reader will notice the President said various things that made one feel that in spite of all he was saying about "all assistance short of war" he would welcome circumstances, or perhaps even help to bring them about, which would enable him to persuade his countrymen that the best way to save themselves from Hitler would be to fight him. For one could not know him well without realizing that beneath his charm, cheerfulness, and beguiling frankness there were hidden regions of thought where ideas were being continually formed, examined, adopted, discarded, or stored ready for use. In that I found the great difference between him and Theodore Roosevelt, whose strength had seemed to lie in a driving simplicity of thought and action.

It was with such thoughts in my mind, coupled with envious comparison between the perspicacity of America's leader and the ignorant obtuseness of our Prime Minister and his principal advisers, that I left the White House after having said goodby for the last time to one of the best of my American friends. I have often wondered whether, if there had been no Pearl Harbor, the President might have found some excuse, such as a submarine attack on one of his patrolling ships, or even upon an American merchant ship, to break with Hitler and commit his countrymen to war. That his country would have followed him I am convinced. Nazi Germany aroused such an overwhelming volume of disgust and fear. For the moment this meant neutralism. But as had been shown in the first German war, even under unconvincing leadership, American public opinion can be changed almost overnight from evasive neutrality to defensive and "offensive" bellicosity. And this time the United States possessed a convincing and popular leader. Before the 1936 election, when many thought Franklin Roosevelt's reelection doubtful, old Colonel House had said to me, "Don't be fooled by the hostility of those who dress for dinner. Franklin has the mass vote behind him."

CHAPTER 23

A Back Seat in the Second War

THE SECOND WAR began for me in a cellar in Birmingham. The cellar was the war room of the regional commissioner for the West Midland Region. The United Kingdom was divided into, I think, twelve regions for purposes of local wartime administration, each with its commissioner and under him a sort of cabinet consisting of the local representatives of the appropriate government departments. I represented the Ministry of Information.

The commissioners were a heterogeneous lot. The three I worked with were an earl, the head of Oxford College, and a retired Indian civil servant. During the Napoleonic War such local emergency administration as was needed was done by the lords lieutenant of the counties. The earl to whom I reported at Birmingham was Lord Dudley, a solid island of aristocratic competence in a sea of "demo-plutocracy." To explain why I was in his war room I must go back a few years.

My free-lancing had got off with a good start. First my book, then my lecture tours in the United States. In the first month back in England after my first tour, I did a lecture at Chatham House, a couple of articles for *The Times,* and a BBC broadcast.

Shortly afterward I became mixed up with the New Commonwealth Society, which was a sort of international version of the League of Nations Union with branches in the appropriate European capitals. Its head and founder was Lord Davies of Llandinan, better known as David Davies, for some time private parliamentary secretary of Lloyd George. Of it I became a vice president and a member of the editorial board. In its publications I opposed appeasement and pleaded for collective security.

I did the same from time to time from the platform for the Liberal Party. Its leaders offered me what they said was a fairly safe parliamentary candidacy. I had seen too much of politics from the sidelines to wish to enter that field. But the overture led to a loose association with the leaders of the party and especially with Archibald Sinclair (Lord Thurso), who seemed to be as fastidiously aloof from the rat race of politics as Lord Grey of Falloden, and with Percy Harris his chief whip, whose house in Chiswick became a hospitable vantage point for observing the Oxford and Cambridge boat race.

Besides Chatham House, the Imperial Defence College and various institutions of that standing made use of me in London. An energetic lecture agent sent me talking around the country; the Workers' Educational Association and the university extension people did the same. I was asked for articles and reviews, and an efficient literary agent placed my unsolicited stuff. I was again to a limited extent practicing my old trade of international correspondent. I contributed syndicated telegraphic dispatches to about ninety newspapers. They were done for the North American Newspaper Alliance, thanks to the good offices of Jimmy James, the managing editor of the *New York Times*. I had, of course, to pull my punches for a polyglot audience that started with the *New York Times* and encircled the globe. But it was a congenial canter in my old field.

All this had to stop if war came. There was the censor for

one thing. What I had heard of the muddling and intrigue involved in the preparatory extemporization of the London emergency war organizations frightened me. So I accepted with alacrity when, some time in the summer of 1939, my old friend Harold Butler told me that he had been appointed commissioner of the Southern Region and asked me to come and help him. He had recently resigned as head of the International Labour Office at Geneva to be the first head of Nuffield College at Oxford. Reading was to be the capital of the Southern Region. I was consequently surprised to be asked, about ten days before the war started, to take on the West Midlands by the Ministry of Information, to which I found I would have to be attached. Harold Butler said that things were in such incoherent confusion in London that he was sure he could wangle my appointment to Reading if I would accept Birmingham for a bit.

My stay in Birmingham was short. The Ministry of Information soon turned out to be the worst of all our improvised war organizations. It became each day more bloated, more unwieldy, and more uncouth. Press and Parliament rose against it. The ministry threw its regional organization to the wolves; why, nobody knew. It did so in the crudest possible manner. I and my colleagues and our subordinates heard of our dismissal on the radio before we received clumsy letters. "You wouldn't sack a housemaid like that," said Dudley when I showed him mine. I sent a long expostulatory telegram to John Hilton, the head of our Home Division, which he said helped him in the fight he immediately started to save us. He was professor of industrial relations at Cambridge and an excellent man but unfortunately did not last long owing to ill health. His civil servant assistant, H. V. Rhodes, was also first-class. He was a tough, gently sardonic Yorkshire man who, like Hilton, knew the provinces, which was more than any of the other top people seemed to do. I moved promptly to Reading whose incumbent had, like many of my other colleagues, resigned in indignation. Hilton asked me to commute to London for a bit to help him with his fight.

Hilton and Rhodes had sensibly made the key to our regional organization a three-party system of local committees and a three-party panel of ministry speakers. They told me and my colleagues that we should find this system difficult to set up, but that there was no way out of it. They were right.

My lecturing in the provinces had not made me realize that England was still as deeply divided as I soon discovered it to be. She was as much "two nations" as she had been when Disraeli wrote *Sybil*. The difference was that the lower nation was now in the majority and knew its mind. It was determined not to have the Conservatives in power whenever and however the war ended. After the First War, reconstruction had fallen to Lloyd George's "hard-faced Parliament" and to the equally hard-faced business community outside it. Wartime promises of social amelioration were not carried out, "homes for heroes" were not built, massive unemployment grew and stayed. This time the postwar reconstruction would be socialistic. Upon that the masses were determined. I was soon aware of this in Birmingham, partly because my Regional Labour adviser, a very good man, warned me and partly because of the nervously hostile attitude of the local Conservatives toward the ministry's three-party plan. In some places they openly opposed having Labour members on our local committees; in others they were more mildly obstructive. They disliked the idea of official Labour Party speakers almost as much, but here it was their representatives in Parliament who were the spearhead of the opposition.

From Reading I found it not too difficult to get our committees going. It was the members of Parliament who were obstructive. I could not make a group of M.P.s, some of whom were personal friends, see that if they refused our authorized Labour speakers they might be overrun by pacifist leftists, of whom there were quite a number busy agitating and trying to infiltrate voluntary organizations and so on. Dunkirk and the fall of France did little to better the situation. We got Duff Cooper, our minister in the summer of 1940, to try to make the backbench Conservative 1922 committee see reason. According to my diary he was "greeted with a regular growl, a low continuous snarling and grumbling," which prevented him making his explanation and appeal.

I started my effort to save our organization with Edward Grigg, an Imperialist Conservative as always, who had been made parliamentary undersecretary of the ministry after the scandal of its inefficiency had caused a reshuffle. He was not helpful. I based my argument for provincial three-party propaganda solidarity upon the need for a national propaganda program. I said that a propagandist without a policy was like a tailor without a pattern to cut to. He said that Labour's opposition to the ministry's plan made home propaganda so difficult; it made everything difficult; it made it almost hopeless to try to put forward a coherent war-aims policy. And anyhow, he said, he seemed to have no authority in the ministry and was not happy there. He moved on before long to more important duties.

I got much the same tune played to me at the Conservative Central Office. Transport House took a rather different line. They felt that they were being ignored by the ministry. The three-party advisory committee that was supposed to give Labour a say in its affairs was not giving them that say. No; for the present, they could not back me in the three-party speaker panel business. They would remain neutral. It was odd, one of them said, to find themselves for once in agreement with Conservative

Central Office. I went to the room of Percy Harris, the Liberal Chief Whip at the House of Commons. There I found Archibald Sinclair and James de Rothschild. My reception was mixed. Rothschild was inclined to be hostile: his agent at Waddesdon had been complaining of a radical pacifist speaker infesting the neighborhood. The other two were not much interested. It did not matter. I do not think this particular problem ever came up in the House of Commons and its urgency died out.

The prevalence of the short war idea was another obstacle to preparedness of all sorts. The First War was going to be short because the financiers thought that neither side could afford to make it long. This war was going to be short because Hitler had gone off at half-cock and a lot of his generals were really against war and him. Or he would run out of supplies; or both. At my club a man of considerable standing who had known Germany as an official said, toward the middle of October, that the war would be over by Christmas. Unless Hitler could secure the active help of Russia he would be in danger from his generals. He would probably bomb us when he felt he was slipping and we should bomb back. The Germans would then collapse; they would stand bombs less well than we should. These ideas that were common were encouraged by some of the German exiles. Rauschning, who had been close to Hitler before they quarreled, "thought that the Nazis were beaten (except Hitler who was by now hardly sane enough to grasp cold truths) but that they would not cave in till they had been smashed by force of arms. The generals and some of the Nazis had peace terms in their minds . . ." Other Germans said much the same. A section of the press helped with nonsense about "Agitated Adolf" and "Gloomy Goering" and so on. It was reported that the Germans were already eating dogs.

It was a fantastic and frightening winter for anybody who had tried to understand Nazi Germany. Not that I was, as I remember it, ever defeatist even at the time of Dunkirk or the fall of France. I cannot say why. Probably memories of the United States and that last afternoon in Washington helped. When Dunkirk was at its height a large packing case arrived for me at the office containing a fine mahogany desk. I took it as a good omen and went out into the town and piled up my car with cases of wine. I felt we were in for a long war. The wine came in useful in the years to come, for one of our functions was beds and dinners for official visitors to Oxford, of whom there were many.

Here are two extracts from my diary giving the sort of thing that was so depressing in spite of one's basic, undefinable hopefulness:

December 9th — Reading.

Dined and slept with the Butlers last night to meet Walter Elliot, a very intelligent man and a member of the Government. He gave us to understand that the profoundest remark about the war was the Prime Minister's dictum that it was a 'political war'.

And yet it is obvious that it will be decided by armed force. And the Government is not even acting upon the political war idea. If it were its propaganda abroad would be less flabby and unimaginative than it is [it got much better later] everywhere from France to the Dardanelles.

The trouble is that decades of almost automatic topdoggery [London had never admitted to itself that the first war had made America the strongest country] and complacency have dulled the sense of danger of our governors. They are like drivers who have driven so long on dry roads that they don't know slippery ones when they see them.

December 3rd — London.

No serious effort to make our war effort 100% effective. Complacency and wishful thinking. One wonders whether all this is not partly due to Chamberlain and Co. thinking that they will be able to polish off the war pretty quickly and repulsing Labour co-operation, so that the Conservatives may be able to say 'alone we did it'.

This perhaps at the bottom of the inadequate war-supply effort. Why, if peace is coming soon, blow in our foreign exchange and foreign investments and why upset industry at home?

Germany, when one penetrates the cloud of wishful judgment, is not doing that sort of thing. She has no mass of unemployed as we have here. She is preparing for a mighty effort on all three elements; her factories are humming. Her foreign trade is better organised than the public here is allowed to know. Our blockade measures will be less effective than we are allowed to believe. Obviously they must be less effective than in the last war; then she was surrounded by enemies; now to a great extent by frightened neutrals.

That complacency was not to be found among wide-awake people in the provinces. There was anxiety and irritation everywhere: over food, for instance (it was before Lord Woolton had been called upon to organize it so magnificently). Why was Birmingham, emptied of many of its inhabitants by the first evacuation, brimming with food, while Oxford, with all its evacuees and refugees, was apparently still upon its peacetime allowance? What about our trade, both export and import? What about the organized manufacture of war matériel on a large scale? And why was our news and propaganda so bad?

After my ministry's home affairs organization had been rescued and my departed colleagues had been replaced, I was sent on a sort of inspection tour of the regional offices. The thing I remember best about it is an evening with Warren Fisher, former head of the Civil Service, then regional commissioner of the Northwest at Manchester. I was surprised to discover him full of abuse of the Civil Service — they seemed to be paralyzed in London; they should be replaced by businessmen. I tried to console him by telling him that President Roosevelt, in recounting his difficulties at the time of the great financial crash, had said that he would have given a lot for a Civil Service like ours.

And here as a pattern of widespread thought during that strange winter of boredom and suspense is another utterance from a very different quarter, from my brother-in-law, Tommy Loyd, who as Lord Lieutenant of Berkshire, Chairman of its County Council, a large landowner, and former Member of Parliament, had facilities of knowing about public opinion:

> Could not London, he asked, do something to relieve the strange boredom which this war which was no war was causing. It was going to make it more and more difficult to enforce war-time regulations. Villages were losing faith in the B.B.C. They listened to the German emissions in English. They wondered and doubted when they heard its lies. But those lies were never contradicted by the B.B.C. and a sort of belief in the German apocrypha was growing up. Could not the B.B.C. take the necessary steps. I told him that I had just seen the B.B.C. newsman about all this and he had said that timidity higher up and the obscurantism of the Fighting Services were his chief trouble. He was very depressed about it.

I told my brother-in-law that people felt just the same at Birmingham, that there was much irritation there at the inadequacy of our news and with the government's war regulations, that they had lost faith in their own Neville Chamberlain, and that after his excellent speech rejecting Hitler's peace offer after the fall of Poland, people wondered who had written it for him.

I recalled the explanation André Géraud, the great French journalist, had given me of our appeasement policy on a visit to England a few years before. "You are asleep," he said. "You are suffering from the effect of your great virtue — your efficiency in crisis. That efficiency comes from your habit of going to sleep between crises. Hence when a crisis comes along, your nerves are fresh and you are able to cope." This time the crisis had come and we were still unable to cope because we were still asleep.

Hitler's seizure of Western Europe including all he wanted of France awoke us, or rather substituted Winston Churchill for Neville Chamberlain. By the conduct of what for a time looked like a forlorn-hope war, by the leadership he gave to the country and the example to the rest of the world, his place high in history is safe. Personally I liked especially the way in which his eyes turned west.

At home, however, I soon realized that our little troubles in forming one regional organization presaged his ultimate discomfiture. In war he was leading magnificently. He would win it whatever the country had to suffer — even a German occupation. But he would not win the peace. He belonged like Lord Curzon to the wrong century. He would not say, as Lord Curzon was said to have exclaimed on seeing troops bathing behind the front in France, "How odd, I always thought that the lower classes were completely covered with hair!" But no more than Curzon was he the person to appeal to the masses when they wanted more privileges and to be assured that the Conservatives of the day understood them better than their fathers had done.

In my experience even Churchill's position as war leader with the masses oscillated considerably. It went high when the Russians joined us and he uttered his wireless greeting. My colleagues and I were told to promote pro-Russian meetings. I remember one in particular, a high-pressure meeting in the town hall at Oxford. The mayor, then a woman, presided, supported by Ronald Tree, Brendan Bracken's parliamentary private secretary and a good ally of mine, and myself on the platform. The Russian ambassador, Lord Beaverbrook, and others sent telegrams, a picturesque member of parliament spoke, as did a fiery local trade unionist. The enthusiasm was tremendous. Tree, as we left the meeting, asked whether I did not find it frightening. Russian meeting followed meeting, packed with those who voted Labour, shunned by those who voted Conservative, boiling with trustful admiration of Russia, distrustful of our predominantly Conservative leadership. America's appearance in the arena in December 1941 rendered victory an ultimate certainty and thus made socialism more than ever worth struggling for.

I had a meeting at Oxford that particularly pleased me. It was an open-air one in the park at Cowley near the Nuffield Works. The speaker was Andrew Rothstein, the correspondent of the official Soviet news agency, a man I had learned to like and respect during my dealings with him in the Foreign Office. The lady mayor presided with my support. Rothstein was at Balliol during the First War and he started his speech as follows, pointing to the hideous barracks which the local regiment occupied behind the park: "About twenty-five years ago I and a band of Oxford undergraduates marched up to those barracks to enlist in another war against another Germany." From a Soviet representative that went down brilliantly with a working-class audience. Children ran loose and some of them climbed onto the back of the platform. Rothstein stayed the night with us. "Was it different from what it would have been in Stalingrad?" we asked him. "Yes," he said, "the children would have been better behaved."

Churchill's standing as a war leader seemed lowest at the time of the Far Eastern disasters of the beginning of 1942. There is a note in my spasmodic diary that in a Reading cinema his appearance and that of Beaverbrook on the screen were received in silence, that of Eden scarcely cheered, and that of Stafford Cripps, a Labour idol at that moment, madly cheered. As to Churchill's position as a politician, shortly afterward I wrote as follows:

> How few realise that an era is ending; that our Empire rushes towards change, destruction perhaps, at a rate undreamed of a few years ago, a few months almost. Rome took its centuries to

decline and fall; with us the one process merges into the other; we are in danger of falling after only really a decade of decline. Does Winston realise this . . . ?

A great leader: courage, eloquence, imagination. But the workers ask: does he understand their problems? Is he the man for social reconstruction? The answer probably is: less than Franklin Roosevelt, like him a Whig aristocrat but with much more socially sensitive antennae.

And a little later on:

> Harold Laski [Chairman of the Labour Party] hopes to persuade the annual meeting of the Labour Party to ask Churchill to formulate his reconstruction plans. But will Churchill go as far as the people want who, as I see it, are simply more and more tired of privilege . . .
>
> Can Churchill escape from his surroundings to the extent of meeting the demand plausibly? No sign of it yet; rather the reverse — his speech the other day about the Conservative party being, as always, the best hope of the nation.

Even the careful and reasonable Labour member of my regional advisory committee at Reading dismissed the Beveridge report, *Social Insurance, and Allied Services,* as "a smoke-screen, to be used by the Tories to conceal repression." When the 1945 election was actually in progress I was mixed up with the opening of a Mulberry Exhibition at Southampton. I asked the major commanding the detachment of engineers working on it how the election was going to turn and he replied, "Why for Labour of course; all my men are voting Labour."

I wondered why people like Beaverbrook sitting in the center of his newspaper web had been unable to forewarn the Prime Minister that being a popular and trusted war leader definitely did not mean that he would be wanted as a peace leader. I wondered, too, whether the blow could have been avoided had he eschewed the Conservative leadership and established himself above the party in 1940. In retrospect, I doubt it.

CHAPTER 24

Americans in England and the Future

M Y OFFICE IN READING was the least repulsive part of Oscar Wilde's Reading Gaol. I had the governor's house with most of my people. The others were parked out by the chaplain's house, etc. There was a large forecourt convenient for our motorcars. Beyond it was the road and then the railway yards, and what were then the Great Western Lines. I had rather a pleasant room looking out on it all. Harold Nicolson on entering it once said, "How odd. Verlaine in his prison at Le Mans found solace in the sound of the shunting; Oscar Wilde in the blue sky." I said that perhaps that was because Wilde's cell looked out at the back.

It was good to be working with Harold Butler, an old and close friend with the same political outlook. We had known each other as children, at school and college, and at Geneva. He had been privy to all my troubles in Geneva and very sympathetic. He understood as nobody in our delegation did how important the press was in the predicament in which we found ourselves. Its secretary was Alec Cadogan, another fellow Etonian and Balliol man, and soon to be head of the

Foreign Office. I always felt during the war that it must have pleased Churchill with his romantic and historical outlook to have had, like his great ancestor, a Cadogan as one of his chief henchmen. Alec Cadogan was a very able public servant and a good friend of mine. But he was the first to admit that he was no "glad-hander"; confrontation with a pressman was embarrassing to him. The way the public mind was working was not his concern. He told me, so far as he could, all I wanted to know loyally and fully and left it at that. Butler on the other hand, with a publicity-oriented mind and all the information of the International Labour Office behind him, was comforting in my inevitably unsuccessful efforts to present Sir John Simon as a statesman.

After nearly three years at Reading Harold's knowledge of publicity was turned to use by the government, which sent him to Washington as chief information officer. Sir Harry Haig who took his place was as helpful as he could be to me, but my real ally in the Regional Commissioner's Office there became Major General R. I. Collins. Jack Collins was a Berkshire figure, a close friend, an amusing and interesting companion, and an invaluable ally when I suddenly found myself responsible for American hospitality, for he had influence with our army and knew how to treat the Americans. Luck was again with me.

So it was with my office. I soon had an excellent staff whose different duties, press, meetings, moving picture vans, etc., and an energetic deputy left me time to travel, attend meetings of our many local committees, and pay almost weekly visits to London after each of which I returned to Reading thanking my stars I was there. We were a happy family. My fellow members of the commissioners' "cabinet" could not have been a better lot. They knew their work. They were kind and helpful to a novice like myself. The Foreign Office had been inclined to look down on the rest of the Civil Service, except the Treasury. I now found that condescension quite uncalled for. My colleagues in Reading were definitely better in rubbing shoulders with the outside, wider world than the average Foreign Office clerk.

Our first serious essay at collaboration came in the summer and autumn of 1940 over evacuation. Here another national, though this time nonpolitical, cleavage plagued us and shamed us. The region was invaded by uncouth, dazed hordes, speaking an almost incomprehensible language, ignorant, unclean, sometimes lice-infested. "All classes are aghast at the state of the evacuated, the lower classes amazed, the upper classes ashamed," exclaimed the regional representative of the Women's Voluntary Service at Birmingham during the first unnecessary evacuation at the outbreak of war. When the bombing started in earnest, what shocked us at Reading was less the state of the evacuees than the failure of London to take advantage of the delay.

In September 1940, I wrote:

The refugees have been taking a good deal of my time. Dame Rachel Crowdy [Commandant of the V.A.D's. on the Western Front in the First War and now looking after the interests of women for the M. of I.] and I went to Oxford, Aylesbury and High Wycombe yesterday. The refugees on the whole are cheerful and patient. Most of them came out haphazardly; Church Societies hired buses which dumped them down; they went to stations and porters told them to get out at Oxford or Banbury or Aylesbury, etc. etc. Or they went where children, left after the first evacuation, were well-treated. London has muddled the whole thing again. No prescience, no organisation. No deep shelters, no evacuation centres, nothing for the East End. Only an immense amount of voluntary work. Newspapers clamp down upon the scandal except the *Daily Herald* and the *Daily Mail*. No that is not fair. The others have protested, but not *The Times* or the *Daily Telegraph*.

Probably this is exaggerated. Anyhow it is an example of the chronic state of exasperation with London in which we in the provinces worked. Lord Woolton with his organization of our food was about the only person who escaped criticism.

Oxford was particularly congested. We crowded masses from the East End into a large empty cinema where community singing and other pastimes were organized. Men would come down to spend nights with their women. "I don't like the situation, sir," said a policeman, "we shall be having some passionate crimes." No passionate crimes occurred. Cheerful toughness again prevailed. Everything, of course, was not perfect everywhere. There were patches of local resentment. I wrote at the time:

> The country (and the towns open to evacuees) resent this swarm of East Enders and bed-wetters — adult bed-wetters, according to the Ministry of Health, are becoming a recognised class. It resents badly behaved children, exigent parents and so on. At Wolverton the comfortable house-proud railway workers refuse to take evacuees.

The better-off refugees could also annoy. Arrogant women in colored trousers and fur coats were not appreciated in Cotswold villages, and small shopkeepers in small towns disliked having their businesses eaten into by urban competitors with sharper minds. But, in restrospect, I think that this great upheaval, helped by television, the radio, and the motorcar, started to bring cities and the rest of the country closer to each other than they would otherwise have been today.

Evacuation problems were followed by the American invasion. Here our organization of voluntary committees and workers again more than justified itself.

American troops, of whom the Southern Region would inevitably have to find room for a large proportion, began to come in the summer of 1942, but the invasion of North Africa for a time lessened the pressure. That was just as well for it was some time before we got our hospitality organization going. At first there was an idea that the regional commissioner should undertake it. In that case I should have looked after it as a special deputy commissioner. It was better, however, that it should go, as it did, to my ministry with our large organization of local voluntary workers.

I was given, too, an admirable team of assistants, a major general, a brigadier, and an Indian civilian, all three just retired and all excellent men. Major General D. G. Johnson was an absolutely ideal choice. He had commanded one of our divisions in France at the beginning of the war; in the First War he had won the V.C., the D.S.O., and the M.C., and he was a most charming man. He cast a spell over the American soldiery. We also had all the help we wanted from the regional commissioner's office. Jack Collins threw himself into the work.

We had to do everything we could to assist American commanders to keep their men happy when off duty. We helped new arrivals to settle down; we found buildings for clubs and the equipment for some of them; we ironed out difficulties, mostly trivial thanks to the good sense and good management of the Americans. By the end of the war we had in the Southern Region helped the American Red Cross find buildings and staff for thirty clubs and had established fifty "Welcome Clubs" of our own. All this would have been impossible but for the good will of everybody concerned, the other government offices at regional level, the local authorities, voluntary societies, our own workers, countless private individuals. When the American Red Cross was in despair about a building for its club at Oxford, the Reading representative of the Ministry of Works gave them a house he had earmarked for his own people in that crowded city. As for private hospitality, some American commanders thought it might be going too far. "It is magnificent, but it is not war," said one high officer wondering if training was not being interfered with. The remark was made in regard to Oxford.

Oxford was our principal center of activity. It swarmed with Americans. There were camps around it and hospitals in it. It was a busy transit center. With Winchester it was our most powerful magnate for sightseers, who never lacked guides. Colleges took officers and doctors into their common rooms. Balliol gave weekly leave courses, as did Reading and Southampton Universities. Rhodes House gave dances; other colleges played their parts. The warden of New College allowed me to bring little parties of officers to Sunday high table. The town hall vied with the university. Private hospitality abounded and was encouraged by the profusion of food guests pressed upon hosts. Other towns, villages, houses from Blenheim Palace downward were equally forthcoming.

The Canadians were not included in our instructions. This together with a remark of a French Canadian to whom I gave a lift irked me at first, "You English," said my passenger, "are a funny race. You hide everything, even your niceness." The remark was elicited by our garden walls, almost unknown across the Atlantic. In point of fact I do not think the omission did much harm. A Canadian of some standing said later on:

The average Canadian might think you a bit effusive to the Americans. But he understands. The Americans need educating and comforting, and also the weight of their number and wealth will win us the war. They need the identification of war aims that your effusiveness provides.

My friend had yet to meet an American officer who regarded the European war as his war. They were over here to win the war for us and then go to the Pacific. Their real enemy was Japan. The Canadians, on the other hand, regarded the European war as their war. They came into it spontaneously at the start because they realized that the Empire was being attacked when Germany, by attacking Poland, attacked us. The Americans on the other hand, were pushed into the war by the Japanese after two years.

A vast mass of American noncombatant troops recruited from the foreign population of the big town certainly had little idea why the Germans had to be fought. They needed the meeting places we helped to provide for them. Without them it was only too often street corners and whistling at girls. But as F. and I discovered, there were exceptions among them, especially in the hospital service — men of education wanting to make the best of their stay in England.

Of the fighting divisions, many of the officers and men appreciated glimpses of our domesticity. They emanated the interested warmth of the ordinary American tourist. They made friends, as was proved by the stream of letters that poured back from the American armies in Europe. Of course there was another side of the picture. Before they arrived I warned our workers that they would find the Americans foreigners in spite of our common, though by no means identical, language. I was glad later on that I had done so. When F. and I were in America we were officially "resident aliens," but actually far less alien than resident. We lost the feeling of being foreigners and became part of the society that surrounded us. It was a little disconcerting, therefore, to discover that we were acutely conscious of the foreignness of the American army in England. There was something larger than life about them. Many, too, were types with whom we had not been familiar in their own country.

They were fresh and we were tired. Their virility and self-assertiveness threw into relief the plight of our crowded, pinched, and warworn community, in spite of their friendly and much appreciated efforts to fit themselves into it. The swollen wallets of the men aroused jealousy when used for girl-snatching (many of the girls did not need much snatching).

Inconsiderate motor-driving by individuals but never by convoys in my experience, a tendency to accept invitations and not turn up, criticism of our trains as cramped, of our roads as medieval, of our motorcars as embryonic, of our girls as badly turned out all caused superficial and sporadic irritation.

We did not like the attitude of the white Americans toward their colored troops. More than once our police had to prevent trouble between our people and white Americans who were rough with the Negroes. The Negroes were by no means unpopular. If they swaggered they were childlike and not overbearing as the white troops occasionally were. They could be unkempt but not aggressively so like some of the whites. Our girls succumbed to the gentleness of voice and manners of some of them. This angered the white Americans as well as our youth. One wondered why the American command, so successful in most of its arrangements, had not confined the export of their colored troops to the Pacific and the Far East instead of risking the repetition on a larger scale of the racial disturbances at home due largely to contrast between French racial egalitarianism in the First War and conditions in the United States. Many American officers felt the same. One in particular I remember. On a savage night of wind and rain my car knocked off their unlighted bicycles two Negroes on the wrong side of the road. I took them, bruised and scared, back to their camp. Its commander was profuse in apologies and regretted that colored contingents had been allowed across the Atlantic.

Differences of behavior and standards came to be largely accepted. Both sides did their best to smooth out difficulties and here we were helped by the excellence of the American organization. Its troops might cause trivial irritations, but in matters of serious discipline such as the care of occupied property they were better than ours. At the end of my term I visited all the local authorities I could with whom I had been doing business. And that was their general verdict.

What permanent effect has that formidable invasion had on the Anglo-American relationship? At this date not a great deal in my humble judgment. Most of the many friendships made were too much of the shipboard variety. I must have spent over a year in Atlantic liners and in all that time I made only two lasting friendships. I imagine that is about a fair average of the permanent results of those ephemeral acquaintanceships.

In 1967 somebody sent me a newspaper cutting from New York that reported that an investigation among college graduates of between twenty-one and thirty years of age showed that quite a number thought that Munich was the name of a German politician or of a German beer, that Dunkirk was an American city or the name of a British peer, that Gestapo was an Italian general or an Italian river, and a concentration camp a place where intellectuals met, or a Boy Scout camp.

Some wartime friendships must of course have endured. Desire to revisit and show to the family wartime haunts must have brought many Americans back here and may have contributed to the replacement of Paris by London as the mecca of American tourists. But I cannot think that the great American wartime inroad has now much, if any, effect upon the day-to-day Anglo-American relationship. The Pacific after all was the principal American war arena.

At the time I did feel that our hospitality efforts and the American response to them paid a good dividend. They helped numberless dazed uprooted men over a lonely and anxious period. They eased some of the problems of their commanders. They afforded many of us personal contact with our friendly invaders that more than made up for the inconveniences inherent in the sudden obtrusion of a large army in our already overcrowded community, efficiently self-supporting though the army was. Also it was the harbinger of certain victory.

I was happy too in what I meant to be the last phase of my active life, to be in a position to repay a small portion of the great debt that F. and I had incurred at the start of it. In spite of the frustrations and anxieties of the First War I look back to the ten years of my correspondentship in Washington as the best in my life — youth, domestic felicity, professional success, good and stimulating friendships. I have mentioned a few of them. One more must come in, namely, that with Henry Adams. The grandson and great-grandson of the Presidents of his name, he was an old man. But as a speculative philosopher he looked forward. He did so gloomily. He used to say that the 1914 war — he died before the end of it — would not be the last war. Inspired, I think, by H. G. Wells, he feared an atomic war in the 1950s. He thought our civilization would survive even that, but feared for it, when the Orient became "tired of sub-sisting upon rice" and, having mastered our methods of fighting, turned upon us. I told this to a Frenchman of standing and perspicacity not long after the last war. "What I fear," he replied, "is that in fifty years' time or so, Africa will be in the hands of the Chinese and that they will be using its slave labour for a final show-down with the United States." Whether he would think the same today I do not know.

As this is written all that seems certain is that the world is in a proper mess. The League of Nations upon which such hopes were placed fifty years ago has failed; the United Nations exists but does not control. The British Empire, which, for all its faults, was a force for stability, has disintegrated, and Common Market or no Common Market, the days when for good or for evil the world revolved about Europe are over. Will the United States persist in taking up the leadership of the Western World? She may not be the confident country she was when I first knew her at the beginning of the century. Yet her "manifest destiny" (the phrase was coined not by Theodore Roosevelt but by a young senator, if I remember rightly) is more obviously there than it was then. Will she persist in taking up that leadership in dealing with Russia and her enigmatic policies, and with the equally aggressive China Henry Adams foreboded? The question is for America to answer but is on all our minds.

On all our minds also is the atomic bomb. I constantly find myself comparing the world today with the Europe of the 1930s. Governments preparing for the worst; business, families, and individuals attempting to live their normal lives. The danger one likes to think is less immediate, save for an accident. In the 1930s it was urgently defined. It came from one man, one system, and one country. Now scattered vast and possibly shifting ambitions and rivalries, material ideological and national, nourish it. They are in some ways ill-defined as well as shifting. Perhaps they will settle down. Meanwhile in regard to the suicidal bomb, there is, of course, one thought from which one can take some comfort. During the last war huge stocks of poison gas were available. But they were never used.

Index